"In a world of endless distraction, Alamar and Schl[...] [...] really matters: family connection. The modern family is [...] [...]e. *The Parenting Project* is filled with helpful, practic[...] [...] that you walk away with strategies you can implement immediately. A must-read book for the busy, modern family."
—**Madeline Levine, Ph.D.**, *New York Times* best-selling author of *The Price of Privilege* and *Teach Your Children Well*

"*The Parenting Project* is rich with practical information and strategies for nurturing the vital art of conversation with our children. Whether it's the incidental chats that build rock solid foundations, the more 'I've got you' ones that soften the sharp edges of the world, to the 'you've got you' chats that help our children discover clarity and courage, conversation is instrumental in building our influence and connection with our children. *The Parenting Project* is a brilliant toolbox for all parents to strengthen their influence and connection with their children, and to make the conversational magic happen."
—**Karen Young**, author of *Hey Warrior* and *Hey Awesome*; founder of *Hey Sigmund*

"Dr. Alamar and Dr. Schlichting have created a useful resource on how to raise healthy, independent adults by providing parents with the tools on how to be respectful listeners and provide unconditional love while creating strong guard rails of limits that will support the journey as it swerves. *The Parenting Project's* easy-to-use prompts and activities will help kick-start daily conversations."
—**Marjo Talbott,** head of an independent day school and parent of two

"Parents play a key role in their kids' adolescent development, and communication should be a top priority, right alongside brushing teeth and studying hard. This book provides a clear and practical road map to starting and continuing regular conversations that will help to develop deeper communication and connection with your teens."
—**Jill Halper, M.D., M.P.H.**, adolescent physician at Valley Community Healthcare

"A warm and compassionate guide to sparking conversations that matter with your child. You don't have to be perfect—and neither does your kid. It's all about learning and growing together."
—**Ann Douglas**, author, *Parenting Through the Storm*

"In the digital age, many of us are struggling to ensure our kids experience the joy of real communication and interpersonal connection. Full of practical tips and ideas, *The Parenting Project* is a step-by-step guide to buil[...]the deep relationships that so many parents struggle with."
—**Kathryn Litwin, M.D.**,

The

PARENTING PROJECT

BUILD EXTRAORDINARY
RELATIONSHIPS WITH YOUR KIDS
THROUGH DAILY CONVERSATION

Amy Alamar, Ed.D., and
Kristine Schlichting, Ph.D.

FAIR WINDS

Inspiring | Educating | Creating | Entertaining

Brimming with creative inspiration, how-to projects, and useful information to enrich your everyday life, Quarto Knows is a favorite destination for those pursuing their interests and passions. Visit our site and dig deeper with our books into your area of interest: Quarto Creates, Quarto Cooks, Quarto Homes, Quarto Lives, Quarto Drives, Quarto Explores, Quarto Gifts, or Quarto Kids.

22 21 20 19 18   1 2 3 4 5

ISBN: 978-1-59233-854-2

33614080815151

Digital edition published in 2019
eISBN: 978-1-63159-588-2

Library of Congress Cataloging-in-Publication Data available.

Design: Laura Klynstra
Cover Image: Shutterstock
Page Layout: Laura Klynstra
Illustration: Shutterstock

Printed in China

The information in this book is for educational purposes only.

MIX
Paper from
responsible sources
FSC® C104723

To our children–

Alex, May, Teddy, Natalie, and Alec—

whom we enjoy conversing with day in and day out.

Thank you for helping us strive to be

the parents you deserve.

CONTENTS

Foreword by Kenneth R. Ginsburg, M.D., M.S. Ed. • 9

Introduction • 13

PART I:
I TALK / YOU TALK: From the Casual to the Difficult • 16
Chapter 1: GETTING TO KNOW YOU • 19

Chapter 2: TYPES OF CONVERSATIONS • 37

Chapter 3: MAKING THE PROJECT WORK • 51

Chapter 4: CONVERSATION STARTERS AND STRATEGIES • 65

PART II:
LET'S TALK: Common Concerns That Come Up Every Day • 82
Chapter 5: OPENING HEART-BASED CONVERSATIONS • 85

Conversation Starters and Prompts:

Emotions • 99

Family • 99

Friendships • 100

Intimate Relationships • 101

Loss and Grief • 102

Self Love • 102

Trust • 102

Chapter 6: NAVIGATING UNCOMFORTABLE CONVERSATIONS • 107

Conversation Starters and Prompts:

Diversity • 117

Divorce/Separation • 118

Fear • 119

Gender and Gender Identity • 119

Sex and Sexuality • 120

Chapter 7: BRAVING DANGEROUS CONVERSATIONS • 125

Conversation Starters and Prompts:

Alcohol and Drugs • 137

Assault and Harassment • 138

Cutting Behavior • 139

Driving • 139

Minor Vices • 141

Suicide • 141

Chapter 8: NURTURING CHARACTER CONVERSATIONS • 147

Conversation Starters and Prompts:

Actions and Behavior • 159

Education and Life Skills • 160

Healthy Habits • 161

Humility • 162

Identity • 162

Integrity • 163

Social Media and Technology • 163

Spirituality • 165

Chapter 9: FOSTERING BRAVE CONVERSATIONS • 169

Conversation Starters and Prompts:

Advocacy and Empowerment • 181

Bullying and Being Bullied • 183

Emotional Health and Anxiety • 183

Independence and Transitions • 184

Mental Health • 186

Taking Risks • 187

Vulnerability • 188

Conclusion • 191

Suggested Resources • 194

About the Authors • 196

Index • 198

THERE IS NOTHING MORE NATURAL THAN OPEN COMMUNICATION, BUT "NATURAL" DOESN'T MEAN EASY. IT TAKES WORK. INVESTMENT. COMMITMENT. PRACTICE.

FOREWORD

· · · · · · · · · · · · ·

There is nothing more protective in the lives of children and teens than healthy relationships with their parents. The unconditional love we give our children tells them that they are worthy of being loved. It launches them into adulthood with the sense of safety and security they will need to get the most out of life's gifts and to successfully navigate its curveballs. Unconditional love doesn't mean we approve of every action or behavior. Rather, it means we care so much that we're not going anywhere. It is about seeing our children the way they deserve to be seen, as they really *are*, not based on a behavior they might be displaying.

We parent best when we stop looking at the child in front of us and begin imagining the 35-year-old we are raising. It is then that we stop prioritizing the happiness that comes with simple fleeting joys (though they can be nice!) and begin imagining how we can foster a sense of meaning and purpose. It is then that we stop thinking about grades and scores and begin thinking about supporting the skills that matter in the real world: perseverance, flexibility, collaboration, and the capacity to elicit and incorporate constructive feedback. It is then that we stop thinking about protection and begin thinking about preparation. It is then that we stop holding independence as our goal and begin grasping that what we really want is to raise children with the secure sense of themselves that allows them to maintain *inter*dependent relationships.

We want to support our children to become their very best independent selves *and* we want to remain in their lives—*inter*dependent on one another—for years to come. The secret to raising children who will benefit from *inter*dependence is to not install control buttons in them during adolescence; this means they know that you have their backs but respect them as individuals. The key is to communicate with them in a way that they learn that sharing their lives with us . . . is a good thing. They need to know that it brings them guidance as well as satisfaction. Joy even. For all of these reasons, open communication within our households is at the root of successful parenting and the tool you will use to guide your children in their journey toward a healthy adulthood.

A starting point is to reject the notion that as our children approach adolescence they need us less, or become uninterested in our thoughts or feelings. We live in a culture in which too many teenagers are met with an eye-roll and too many parents are told to "hang on tight" through the teen years. Adolescence is to be celebrated as a time of tremendous growth, not survived as a period to be gotten past. We know that teens care deeply about their relationships with their parents and look to us as a valuable source of guidance. We must create, starting at very early ages, the expectations that our homes are safe spaces in which we express our feelings, gain guidance . . . and support and enjoy each other. We want our homes to be the place where our children learn "that sharing their lives with us . . . is a good thing"—a place where the seeds of lifelong *inter*dependence are sown.

There is nothing more natural than open communication, but "natural" doesn't mean easy. It takes work. Investment. Commitment. Practice. It needs to become a pattern and a skill-set. The brilliance of *The Parenting Project* is that it offers the framework and strategies to build the kind of meaningful relationships within your family that will last a lifetime. Perhaps as importantly, what our children learn and live in our homes prepares them to have successful relationships in the workplace as well as loving and mutually respectful relationships within their future families.

KENNETH R. GINSBURG, M.D., M.S. Ed.

Author of *Building Resilience in Children and Teens: Giving Kids Roots and Wings*
and *Raising Kids to Thrive: Balancing Love with Expectations and Protection with Trust*
Co-director of The Center for Parent and Teen Communication,
The Children's Hospital of Philadelphia
www.parentandteen.org

"INTENTIONS COMPRESSED INTO WORDS ENFOLD MAGICAL POWER."

DEEPAK CHOPRA

INTRODUCTION

• • • • • • • • • • • • •

*W*elcome to *The Parenting Project*. We wrote this book because we know that conversation is the ideal tool to help you develop a deep and long-lasting relationship with your kids, but we also know that talking with tweens and teens can be a challenge. We want to help you kick-start the habit of talking with your kids so it becomes a natural part of your day and something you both enjoy.

We all lead busy lives, and a lot gets lost in the shuffle. Often, we may feel like we are short on time when we need it most. However, the time you invest in building a habit of conversation with your child pays rich dividends. With your attention, you provide the love and comfort your children need and yearn for. You also provide, through conversation, a place for them to firm up their own beliefs and test their ideas. When you share your ideas, your child processes them and often adopts them, at least early on. And, through a back-and forth in which you are truly asking and listening as well as sharing your own thoughts, you can help your child develop her own ideas and stand firm in her principles.

ABOUT THE PARENTING PROJECT

In *The Parenting Project*, we've broken the art of talking with kids into simple strategies that draw on proven educational and psychological concepts, and we pair those with easy-to-use activities and prompts that help you start meaningful conversations with your children. Research in neuroscience shows that people learn best when they are introduced to a concept via an activity and then have time to reflect on the activity. This process increases engagement, activity, and brain stimulation. Based on i-therapy—a method Dr. Schlichting developed to introduce conversation that builds positivity, resilience, goal setting, and independence with our children—the project approach helps you prepare for conversations and confrontations and also jump in on the fly when necessary. i-therapy is action-based and focused on solutions that create real-time changes and strength within the individual.

The Parenting Project invites you to take a deep dive into your conversations with your kids, with the goal of helping you nurture and sustain a meaningful relationship with them. And for your kids, understanding how to talk about a range of topics, from light to serious, and practicing the art of conversation will also help them build relationships outside your immediate family. This book provides you with the background you need to start and foster those conversations as well as practical strategies for continuing them as your child grows. You will be talking with your kids about lessons you've learned, values, wishes, times you cried the hardest, sex, drugs, and, you bet, rock 'n' roll!

There's no time like the present. Jump in and start talking. Get comfortable and lean into conversations with your child. Ideally, you have a strong bond with your child and will find it easy to make daily conversations a focus of your parenting. If not, don't despair; you can work on your relationship and get to your goal. The more you normalize conversation between you and your child, the better your relationship will be and the easier it becomes to engage when you need to. Best of all, you will enjoy each other's company.

Conversation will not always come easily, but we help you get started. In Part 1, we'll introduce a variety of conversation types, offer general tips for starting conversations and keeping them going, and address some common concerns and challenges. In Part 2, we will dive into the types of conversations you may be having with your child, discussing the importance of the topics as well as strategies for engaging on the specific concerns. Each chapter in Part 2 includes activities that help you talk with your child about the topics in the chapter. Following the activities are specific prompts for the more challenging conversations, concluding with a "Conversation in Action" that draws from real-life scenarios.

This book is designed to be used flexibly, so you may choose an activity to start the conversation or you may decide to focus on one of the prompts in Part 2 to get yourself off and running.

Think about *The Parenting Project* this way: If you plan to run a road race this spring, it is not enough to buy the sneakers and the outfit, you must actually start running (and maybe even walking first, working your way up to a jog and then a sprint). The same principle is true of emotional or psychological change. If you want to build a deeper relationship with your kids, you can't simply buy the book, you must do the work. The activities and hands-on approach will help you to do the work required to build a daily habit of conversation. Together, the exercises function as a behavior change manual, showing you how to create a healthy, functioning relationship with your child.

ABOUT US

In addition to being proud professionals in the fields of education and psychology, we are proud parents. Throughout the book, we share what we know from our work and what we have found in our own personal stories and those of friends and clients, though we have changed names to protect the individual's privacy. We worked to make this book as easy to read as possible, so we also simplified our personal stories by writing them from the singular first-person point of view, reflecting our combined experience.

While there is no one way to relate to your child, we do know that conversations lead to deeper relationships, and we use that premise to help you build a bond with your child that will see you through the teen years and beyond. We hope that you will find *The Parenting Project* a vital first step in starting this new journey with your child. We will be right beside you through your conversations, and we hope you will lean on this guide as you would a good friend.

PART I

· · · · · · · · · · · · ·

I TALK / YOU TALK:

FROM
THE CASUAL
TO
THE DIFFICULT

You've picked up this book because you want to start conversations with your child that will help define and enhance your relationship. In Part 1, we'll lay the groundwork for these conversations, focusing on the benefits of talking daily. We'll walk you through suggestions for starting meaningful conversations, giving practical tips on where, when, and how.

Chapter 1 reinforces the basic need for conversation and includes the beginning steps of the project—a guided conversation to get you and your kid talking—and identifies some of your strengths and concerns. Chapter 2 explores the different types of conversations you will have, linking to the topics discussed in depth in Part 2. Chapter 3 helps you establish a habit of talk in your home and addresses common concerns, while Chapter 4 offers valuable conversation starters to get your talks rolling.

"THE ATTITUDE BEHIND YOUR WORDS IS AS IMPORTANT AS THE WORDS THEMSELVES."

ADELE FABER AND ELAINE MAZLISH

Chapter 1

GETTING TO
KNOW YOU

• • • • • • • • • • • • • •

"*C*an I talk to you?" my daughter asked one evening as I was finishing a work email. I didn't think much of it and said, "Sure." Then she said, "In private?" Uh-oh. I could feel my heart beating, hear the throbbing in my ears. What did I do? What did she do? What's wrong?

While my daughter happily participates in conversations, she rarely initiates them—and this sounded serious. I needed to finish my email but I was having trouble focusing. We went to her room and she sat on her bed and looked at me, eyes wide. We just sat.

Eventually, she shared that she had thought she'd done well on a few tests and assignments but that her scores were not what she wanted. She was disappointed in herself. I sat there, relieved. I care about her grades, but I was ecstatic that *she* cared about her grades. And I was thrilled that she came to me. "Okay," I responded. "What can I do?" A parent's natural instinct is to jump in and fix a problem, but I soon realized that I didn't need to do anything. I just needed to be there with her and help her think through her next steps.

In parenting, the goal is to raise an independent adult, and it's often hard to keep that in mind when you're in the midst of it, dealing with an adolescent. We want kids to do their own thing, take risks, and find themselves—however, we would prefer that they do it the way we want. But following parents' instructions every step of the way is not what growing up is about. While kids will not take the path we set out for them every time, we can still remain a strong influence in our children's lives. The best way to keep your influence in your child's life is to stay connected.

PUSHING BOUNDARIES

When you think back, how do you remember the experience of growing up? What were your concerns? Whom did you go to for advice or to talk things through? If you went to your parents, why? What solidified your relationship and how did they maintain that trust with you? Do you and your child have a similar trusting relationship? And if you didn't go to your parents, why not? What was the barrier? Have you created a similar barrier with your child? How can you start to break it down?

A child's job as she grows up is to push boundaries and try new things. We should expect kids to make poor choices and do things we'd prefer they not do. Our job is to keep calm and carry on. So when your child acts out, makes a mistake, or gets caught red-handed, it's your job to understand that her behavior is likely not a personal stab at you but rather part of the process of growing up. And while it's your job to help your child see the error of her ways by establishing logical consequences, be sure to talk with her about her decisions and their ramifications. This conversation provides her with context and understanding, and sets her up to make a different decision next time—or to at least better understand her choice and its likely outcome. During conversations about choice-making, acknowledge your child's feelings and perspective—her concerns, anxiety, anger, sadness. What drove her decision?

Teens and tweens often experience strong emotions that they are not prepared to handle in the moment. So acknowledge their feelings and realize that understanding does not mean you have to celebrate the emotion or the decision that resulted from it. Rather, you are showing your child that you are trying to understand where she is coming from.

Acknowledgement doesn't mean you have to refrain from punishing your child if she has transgressed. For example, if your daughter was angry and took the car out after curfew to blow off steam, then she should face the consequences—perhaps she should lose car privileges for a set period of time. But the consequence comes after you've discussed her feelings, her decisions, and healthy alternatives. The goal is to open a conversation so you can better relate— so you can understand why she reacted as she did and she, in turn, can understand why you are upset by her behavior.

If you develop a habit of conversation, you will maintain influence in your child's life, and she will have the opportunity to see things through your eyes. Sure, she will make up her own mind, but she will have the benefit of your perspective. We all come to conversations with our own unique viewpoint—and so do our kids. You might think you're simply making small talk, but then all of a sudden you're in a full-on debate. Don't assume your child agrees with your political or social views, and don't be surprised when your child argues vociferously about something that doesn't matter all that much to you.

Examine your own hopes, fears, concerns, and motivations so you have insight into your approach. Getting to know ourselves and our kids is the best start to understanding how we deal with conversations. Use the parent-child interview questions later in this chapter to share your views and experiences and to get to know your child. You'll start to notice patterns in your interactions, and you can use those patterns to replicate what works well and to adjust what doesn't. For example, if you tend to approach conversations with an open question and your child responds, continue doing that. And if you start conversations with a strong opinion and your child shuts down quickly, try a gentler tactic.

TACKLING THE PROJECT

If you want to be an influencer in your child's life, you need to invite your child in and listen to him. We can't just tell our kids our values, we need to illustrate where our values come from and share the stories that fostered those values. In establishing a strong bond with your children, you increase the chance of them coming to you with the good, the bad, and the ugly. You want them to celebrate their wins with you and share their funny experiences, but you also want them to come to you when the going gets rough.

When we are in the midst of a discussion, especially a heated or emotional one, we can overthink and overreact—or we may underthink our response, suggesting we are not as invested in the topic at hand. While you're trying to balance overthinking and underthinking your next decision, your tweens and teens are defining themselves in every moment, also overthinking and underthinking their decisions.

At the same time, adolescents are trying to hold steady in the face of all the emotional and physical changes they are experiencing, as well as handle intense peer pressure. Kids are constantly balancing the desire to stick out and to fit in, both at the same time. This can feel like an impossible task, so do your best to empathize with your tween or teen, and understand how emotionally loaded some of his responses may be.

PARENT-CHILD Q&A

Find time with your child and let him know why you want to sit down together. You can say something along the following lines: "I'm reading a book about conversations and how important it is to have them with your kids. It's a project with a few activities to get us talking. I am so excited to start having more conversations with you and really learning more about who you are. In the first activity you can ask me lots of questions, and I will ask you questions as well. My hope is that it will be fun and we will both learn a lot." Then share the book with your child and the directions for the first part of the parent-child interview. Take notes as the two of you talk, and then debrief together.

Directions for child: Find time with your parent so you can learn more about him or her. Understanding your parents as people helps you see where they are coming from and why they think and feel as they do. Choose five to ten questions from the list that follows, then ask your own follow-up questions if you have any. Take note of what interests you. After getting answers to the questions you've chosen, take a break and return to the list later or on a new day. When you have finished interviewing your parent, let him or her interview you. Share with your parent(s) what you learned about them, and, after they interview you, talk about what you learned about yourself.

QUESTIONS TO ASK YOUR PARENT(S):

What is your earliest memory? What was your childhood like?

What were you good at in school?

What were your weaknesses?

Did you participate in activities or clubs? What were they?

Do you still do any of the activities that you did when you were my age?

What would you say your current hobbies or interests are?

Who lived in your home when you were my age?

Did you feel the rules were fair or unfair in your home when you were my age?

What person were you closest to when you were my age?

What kind of jobs have you had in the past? How did you get them?

What do you find most difficult about your life?

What do you find most enjoyable about your life?

What would you consider your greatest strengths?

What would you consider your greatest weaknesses or challenges?

If you had three wishes granted what would they be?

What do you daydream about?

What persons, ideas, or forces have been most useful or influential to you in the past?

When are you happy?

What would you like to do more of?

What would you like to do less of?

What do you want to change about yourself?

Directions for parent: Now it's time for you to interview your child. After asking five to ten questions, take a break and return to the list later or on a new day. Come up with your own follow-up questions if you have any as you go through the interview, and take note of what interests you. Feel free to do this over a few days if you want to get through the whole list. Share with your child what you learned about him/her, and talk about what you learned about yourself.

QUESTIONS TO ASK YOUR CHILD:

What is your favorite thing in your life? What gives you joy?

What is the most frustrating thing in your life right now? What is your greatest challenge?

What is your favorite/least favorite subject in school? Why?

Overall, do you like school?

How are your relationships with your teachers?

What are your relationships with your classmates like? Describe someone you like, and tell me why. Describe someone you don't like and say why.

Do you get into arguments or fights with other kids? How do the fights usually start and end?

Do you have a girlfriend or boyfriend?

Do you ever get into trouble in school?

Do you worry about school?

If you could change one thing about school, what would it be? How could you make this happen?

What is your earliest memory?

Are the rules in our home fair or unfair? Why?

Who understands you best?

Who do you best identify with at home? What are some things you have learned from this person?

If you could change something in our home, what would it be? What are some ways to make this happen?

If you were to describe yourself to a someone who did not know you well, what would you say?

What would you like to do in the future? What are your plans to achieve these goals?

What makes you happy/mad/sad/scared?

What do you worry about?

How do you feel most of the time?

Complete these sentences:

The most important thing about me is...

The most important thing in my life is...

The best thing in my life is...

The worst thing in my life is...

My greatest strengths are...

My greatest difficulties or challenges are...

I daydream about...

If I had three wishes granted I would ask for:

1.

2.

3.

If I could change one thing about myself, it would be...

HOW YOU RESPONDED

You and your child should both take some time to reflect on what you talked about in your interview by responding to the following prompts:

Have you learned anything new about yourself?

Have you learned anything new about your child/parent?

What were your favorite questions to answer?

What were the most interesting things you learned about your child/ parent?

Was there any part of the interview that felt awkward or challenging? If so, what was it, and why do you think you felt that way?

What were you excited to share?

What did you resist sharing?

Share these answers with each other and think about new questions to ask about the other person's answers. These questions are merely springboards to deep-level conversations and continued sharing.

Parents: Don't be afraid to be vulnerable with your answers and reveal things that are important, embarrassing, or sensitive. You are modeling for your child how to develop a bond with another person. This is an important skill to develop and replicate in any long-term relationship. You are helping your child learn how to create a strong foundation for a relationship.

As you review the way you responded to the interview, consider your own conversational strengths and challenges. Think as well about the right environment for your conversations. Take a moment to consider:

➤ When is a good time to talk with your child (time of day, before/after eating, during another activity, etc.)?

WHO CAN YOU TRUST?

Begin a conversation about the characteristics of trust and the actions of trustworthy people. Ask your child what makes somebody a person she can trust. Jot down your child's thoughts in list form. After reviewing her answers, write your own list, then talk with her about the two lists. Can she identify people she trusts? Why does she trust them?

Make sure your child knows that if she has doubts about a person's trustworthiness, she shouldn't ignore her gut instinct. She can, and should, come to you. Those doubts could be about a friend, a teacher, a coach, or another adult.

If there are marks of trustworthiness you look for that are not on her list, ask her if you can add them to her list. To get you started, here are some descriptors you might consider including:

Empathetic—does the person empathize with you? Do they take time to feel what you are feeling?

Good listener—does the person truly listen to what you have to say?

Honest—has this person ever lied to you?

Responsible—does this person honor commitments?

Open—does this person share personal stories?

Strong character—does this person have good relationships with friends and family? Does this person follow through on promises he or she makes?

Compassionate—do you feel this person truly understands you? Does this person care about you?

➤ Are there environmental supports that help create a sanctuary for talking and sharing (such as blankets, soft lighting, a quiet space with no TV in the background, etc.)?

➤ What factors make it hard to talk with your child (approaching a difficult subject, disclosing personal information, learning new things about your child, facing disappointments, etc.)?

➤ What do you do well when you talk with your child (make eye contact, listen, move the conversation along, open up, etc.)?

HOW YOU REACT

It's important to know the way you are likely to react in different situations. Of course, each situation is unique, but identifying your typical reactions can help you have better conversations. For example, if you tend to respond impulsively, you might work on developing some phrases to fall back on, like, "My knee-jerk reaction is. . . But give me some time to consider"—and make an effort to think through your responses more. Alternatively, if you lean toward processing your thoughts and your child appears to be looking for a more immediate response, you might work on ways to respond that buy you time to think things through. Also, knowing how your child is likely to react will help you time conversations and tailor your responses for true engagement rather than just talking at one another.

Are you calm and even-tempered most of the time? A relaxed approach can help you ease into conversation. If you find you are quiet during conversations or are too mild-mannered, work on modeling vulnerability and openness. By using the conversation starters and prompts in Part 2 of this book and opening up to your child, you create a framework that he can apply in his own life to create meaningful connections with others. Research shows that these deep connections create lasting happiness in our lives, and this is the legacy we all want to leave our children.

A subdued reaction or consistently laissez-faire attitude can signal to your child that you are not concerned or that the topic at hand is not as important to you as he might want it to be.

Do you tend to get anxious easily or are you quick-tempered? This can mean you are passionate and care very deeply, which your child likely picks up on. But an outsized reaction on your part can also trigger arguments or stifle conversation. If you worry about this or find it happening, realize that you need time and space to process the conversation, ideally before you engage.

Sometimes you don't have the luxury of taking a time out or finding a quiet spot. In those cases, look within yourself and talk through your mood as best you can. Remember to take breaks if you feel overwhelmed or emotional.

Think before speaking and check any need you have to control the situation. It is important to have a space for your child to unwind and come undone at times, and this is an uncontrolled reaction. It's important that your child knows he can come to you and trust you. If you overreact or judge quickly, you may unwittingly signal for the child to stop the conversation before it gets out of control. Know yourself, and if you tend to overreact, or if certain situations trigger a strong reaction or anxiety, identify your tendency and work on it when you're feeling in control.

How quick are you to offer an opinion or judgment? Sometimes advice can be helpful, but it can also stifle your child. Avoid offering your thoughts right off the bat (don't worry, you can and should offer your opinion once you've heard your child out). Most importantly, listen. You can't know what your child is thinking, but you can listen to what he tells you and try to interpret as best you can. Ask clarifying questions. Once you're engaged in conversation, your child might even ask for your opinion. If you do feel the urge to share and can't stop yourself, be sure to frame it as your opinion and say that you simply feel compelled to share it.

HOW YOU LEARN

Understanding the way you and your child learn will help you engage in conversations more fully. Are you able to simply sit and listen, or do you prefer to be active, walking, knitting, or cooking? Do you ask questions when you're confused or just gloss over things you don't understand?

Knowing your learning strengths and challenges will help you identify areas to focus on in your conversation. For example, I am not an auditory learner and I can gloss over things I don't understand or that don't interest me. That's something for me to recognize when talking with my kids, so I make an effort to focus and catch myself when I drift.

As I was driving my daughter to her skating lesson one day, she began talking about some fan fiction she was reading. While I love that she was reading, I had no interest in the fan fiction, let alone the complicated story she was relaying. I tried to pay attention but my mind wandered. She must have been talking for fifteen minutes before I realized she was talking about ships, and that boats had nothing whatsoever to do with what she had been describing. So I stopped her to clarify, only to learn that "ships" are "relationships" between two superheroes. The conversation that ensued was hysterical, as we talked about what would happen if these two superheroes got together, or what about those two…. That led to a conversation about personalities and what works well for relationships. If I hadn't made the effort to tune in, I would have missed this opportunity to talk at length about relationships with my daughter. And now we often refer to that conversation to lighten the mood when we're talking about serious relationships.

Understanding your own tendencies and mindset allows you to see where you shut down opportunities and where you are open to new experiences. What is your mindset like with regard to parenting? Do you focus on limitations when your child experiences a setback? Or do you try to find the area for growth and learning?

Psychologist Carol Dweck defined the terms "growth mindset" and "fixed mindset." A growth mindset is the belief that effort and learning can lead to talent and skill. A fixed mindset is the belief that talent and skill are innate. People with a growth mindset tend to persevere through disappointment and frustration because they believe they can achieve a goal even when it doesn't come naturally or right away. They worry less about never being able to "get it" and focus more on what they need to do to improve. People with fixed mindsets lean toward giving up or cheating to get ahead. People can express different mindsets at different times and in different facets, and growth mindsets need to be developed.

Supporting a growth mindset for your child will help her develop resilience and persistence. One of the biggest features of the growth mindset is praising effort rather than the outcome. As your child answers questions you ask, you may think she is not staying on topic or answering your question fully. Focus not on the content but on the process and the journey of getting to know each other better. It is normal for children to get off topic, talk tangentially, and respond emotionally to questions—and these are all good things. The idea behind the interviews, conversation starters, and prompts is to use them as a template to build your own "house of conversation"—so don't worry about sticking to the script. Remember, while these talks may feel like an emotional risk for you and may feel unnatural at first, they are also an emotional risk for your child, so be extra supportive, kind, and accepting.

HOW YOU ENGAGE

Understand that learning to have productive conversations is a process, and the way you feel about the conversation will vary with the topic, your mood, and your perspective. Having good conversations with your child is about knowing how to approach and engage—it's not about ending every conversation without conflict. Clashing opinions, the challenge of understanding each other, and the messiness of dealing with each other's feelings are all a part of the process. Enjoy that process with the knowledge that you will not always enjoy the conversation.

Take the opportunity to talk with your children when they are having a good day, but also when they are having a bad one. Whether they are hurt emotionally or physically, relate their pain to a broader life experience. Talk about times when you faced a similar challenge, and help them make a connection to you; tell them about a time when you were hurt, when you failed, or when you were frustrated. What did you do?

Life can throw a mess of challenges your way, and it's great to talk about what you've done in the past to face them, using the lessons you learned to help your

WHEN SOMEONE BREAKS YOUR CHILD'S TRUST

Every day, kids find out that someone said something behind their back. All too often these days, the nastiness is posted online for many more to see. How do you cope when that happens?

Get clarity. If you heard about the incident from your child, ask him for the details. If you heard about it from someone else or noticed the activity on your child's social media account, follow up with your child for details. Don't assume this is a bigger deal than it is.

Assess how upset your child is. If he appears to be shrugging it off, follow his lead. If he seems upset about the incident or wants to address it, help him do that, using the following suggestions.

Discuss options. Talk with your child about his options. He could report the incident, approach the person/people who posted the offensive comment, identify other people to hang out with, or ignore it. Ask your child what results he wants to come out of this incident. Does he want it to go away, to tell the other person off, or to establish boundaries with the person? Whatever your child's choice, role play what he will say or do, and offer to accompany him if appropriate.

Lean on support. Identify someone in your community who you and your child trust that can help to remedy the situation. This could include a school counselor or administrator, a therapist, your pediatrician, or a social worker. Depending on the level of exposure, consider filing an official report with the school or police department.

Continue to check in. Check in regulary and also be sensitive to changes in his mood, behavior, friends, sleep, and eating, in case something changes.

Talk about trust. Open up a conversation about what it means to trust someone. Did your child trust the person who made the offence? What signs did your child see or miss? What can he look for in his relationships to identify people he can truly trust?

child face challenges in the here and now. Sometimes, families adopt a motto or philosophy to live by, and these family mottos can come in handy when confronting daily crises. One family I worked with used as their motto the expression, "Everybody has to try." This way, while you may not get "it" right (whatever "it" is), you have to try. My father-in-law would say, "Some days you eat the bear, and some days the bear eats you." While I've never found that to be helpful in solving a problem, it is somewhat comforting in that it helps to acknowledge my kids' feelings on a less-than-perfect day.

STORIES THAT BIND US

As humans, we are all vulnerable, and acknowledging that rather than hiding it can help us unlock the door to engagement with our children. Telling your own childhood stories helps you enter into the conversation, and this approach is generally more successful than asking direct questions that may be met with one-word answers. Your children are more interested in your personal stories than you might think—especially the embarrassing and colorful ones.

Think for a moment about Hollywood and the most compelling stories told on the big screen. These are not all rainbows and unicorns—they are about big personalities who overcome big obstacles in one way or another. Share your most captivating stories, the ones where you triumphed or failed in a dramatic way. You may be surprised to learn that your kids will actually think more highly of you when you share your vulnerable moments, and they will begin to see themselves in your stories. They will be interested hearing about your resilience, perseverance, failures, and heartbreak.

Our brains are expertly built to understand and hold stories in long-term memory. Stories incite emotion, not logic. And emotion, especially in tweens and teens, drives behavior. Stories inspire people to take action and change behavior, and the most powerful ones you can tell your children are your own hard-earned stories. Your kids actually do want to get to know you.

Learning how you overcame obstacles and developed grit will help your child see that he is not alone in his struggles. The difficult things we have overcome helped us build resilience, and sharing those tough moments and our strength with our children will help them build a framework for their own resilience.

CONNECTING AND RECONNECTING

If you already have a strong connection with your child, *The Parenting Project* will help you continue and bolster it. If you once had a close connection and feel that you are losing it as your child hits the tween or teen years, now is the time to rekindle that relationship. Your tween or teen is likely discovering a new part of himself as he grows up, and you can get to know that new dimension of your child through conversation.

If you have never felt a strong connection with your child, don't spare a moment in getting meaningful conversation going. Read through this book and highlight questions you would like to ask your child. Beginning with lighter subjects may be best for some kids; however, you may get a stronger response if you start with the dangerous or uncomfortable topics first. It really depends on the personality of your child and the relationship you currently have.

If something came between you and your tween or teen, your best bet is to deal with that situation head-on as you begin this project. *The Parenting Project* requires trust, honesty, and openness, so work on building those elements back into your relationship. Don't waste time feeling ashamed that the relationship isn't perfect—no one's is—and kudos to you for paying attention to your child's emotional health. Stay focused in the present and keep digging to find out more about your child and how he operates in the world. Using the activities and conversation starters, you'll be embarking on a journey into conversation that will help you build a profound relationship with your child.

"I SUPPOSE IT IS TEMPTING, IF THE ONLY TOOL YOU HAVE IS A HAMMER, TO TREAT EVERYTHING AS IF IT WERE A NAIL."

ABRAHAM MASLOW

Chapter 2

TYPES OF
CONVERSATIONS

• • • • • • • • • • • • •

*W*hile I was in the midst of writing this book, my daughter burst into my office, very upset. "I've been calling for you for ten minutes!" she wailed. I answered, "I'm working. I'm busy. What do you need?" My daughter declared angrily, "Never mind now, I figured it out myself," and stormed off. She did need me, but not to figure anything out; she needed her mother's attention and support. She just needed me there in that moment. And even though it was an angry exchange, it was one that offered an opportunity for connection. My daughter did, in fact, get what she needed; it just didn't look like what she expected.

Have you ever noticed that your adolescent tends to take out her frustrations on you more than on others? Do you sometimes wonder if she has been saving that outburst or sullen look for you all day? Well, you're not crazy. Kids often let their true colors fly when they are feeling safe, and the good news is that, if they are more short-tempered with you, you've likely created a safe place for them to be themselves and let off steam when they need to.

It's not always easy to see these moments coming, so it's good to learn to look for a few clues and to keep your eyes and ears open. Look for telltale signs that a mood might be coming on: Is your child grumpy when she's hungry or when there is a pile of homework? Is she fragile when a test is coming or after a loss on the soccer field? You won't be able to predict all the moods, but you can anticipate some and plan for them by being understanding of the triggers. On top of that, you can talk with your kid about how to manage emotions when they come on strong. In this chapter, we will look at the different types of conversations crucial for building relationships and keeping kids safe and connected to you.

USING CONVERSATIONS TO CLARIFY PERSPECTIVE

When entering into conversations with your kid, acknowledge and validate her feelings. This requires you to listen and process what she is saying and shows her that you are truly listening. An approach like, "It sounds like you're frustrated. Do you want to talk about it?" often works better than, "You're in a mood today. What's going on with you?" Acknowledging and validating feelings is not blanket permission for your child to behave badly, but a way of understanding her perspective and sharing in the conversation. By reflecting or mirroring your child's emotional state without judgment, you are offering a safe place for your child to unload her worries, fears, and struggles. When possible, start fresh in a conversation and don't rehash the past. Even if you feel like you're having the same conversation over and over, do your best to start anew.

While we all approach conversations with our own assumptions and beliefs, you should make every effort to understand how your beliefs affect what you think and say. Try not to make assumptions about what your child says or does, or you could steer the conversation in an unproductive direction. For example, my son shared his class schedule with me, looking for my approval. He had thought about his courses and had made informed decisions. I jumped in and suggested a different choice—and while I may have had a good point about the calculus class, I could have been more effective if I had started with some questions and learned more about my son's reasoning before making suggestions. Soon we were arguing rather than discussing the schedule rationally. Recognizing that he was getting frustrated, I stepped back and asked a few questions. We ended in agreement about his schedule, but I wish I had done a better job of clarifying his perspective before making suggestions.

It is easy to internalize your child's negative feelings and think that her bad attitude is about you. The best approach is to be curious about your child's mood, ask questions, and move on. For example, if your child stares without responding to you and you assume she is angry with you, check in. She could be scared or ashamed and doesn't have the words to express what concerns her. Offer some opening words like, "It seems like you're upset or focused on something else. Can you tell me what's up?" This will also help you to determine what type of conversation you're about to get into.

GETTING A SENSE OF THE CONVERSATION

Conversations will sometimes be ordinary, and sometimes they will be extraordinary. Sometimes, they will take a turn and surprise you. You may be talking about one thing and then learn something completely new about your kid. This chapter outlines the five types of conversations you will encounter most and identifies specific strategies for approaching them. While there are certainly more than five conversation types, we focus on the most important ones—those that will help your tween/teen develop into an aware, resilient, and strong kid. Many kids already have information on these topics from various sources, including social media, school, friends, siblings, and TV/movies or other pop culture outlets.

When I had the "sex talk" with my daughter, for example, she said, "Oh, Mom, we did this in school already." This is your prompt to add a colorful story about how you learned about the "birds and the bees." If your child believes that this talk may be interesting, she will be more likely to pay attention.

Conversations can get emotional, and when the talk is uncomfortable or about dangerous situations, teenagers may back off or go quiet. In each of the five areas of conversation, honor your child's role. A conversation is an exchange, and it requires input from both parties. Listening is about understanding and empathy. True listening may be silent and does not follow an agenda. This means you don't need to jump in and steer the conversation. Aim to hold off on judgment and try to be neutral. As parents, we can model this important behavior for our children. Be sure to validate your child's opinion, concerns, and ideas. Remember, validation is not a general stamp of approval but signals appreciation and respect. It makes your child feel heard.

Like toddlers, adolescents go through major psychological and physiological changes, and they need support. Transitions can be both exciting and challenging—your child is growing and developing physically, intellectually, and emotionally, and can't always control herself. Adolescents' decision-making abilities (executive functioning) are not fully developed, and at times, impulsivity, social pressure, and adrenaline take over and they make bad choices.

When your child was a toddler, she wanted to do everything herself, and while it took patience to let her put on her own shoes, encouraging her independence paid off in the long run. Now she still wants to do it herself, but the situations are bigger and riskier. As an adolescent, your child has new ideas and a sense of adventure. Support that independence, just as you did when she was small. Instead of using transitions against her ("You're not old enough yet," or, "You don't know; I have experience."), try celebrating this newfound independence ("I'm so excited for you to try the new school—how exciting, but it might also be scary," or, "Your first date, wow! How do you feel about it?"). Approach your child from a place of curiosity rather than judgment and superiority. Be curious about what her experiences are and how she feels. Try to see things through her eyes to gain a deeper understanding and acceptance of her place in her ever-changing world.

No matter the conversation, keep an open mind and be a good listener. We'll talk about general strategies for broaching conversations in Chapter 4 and break each type down further in later chapters. As you read through the types of conversations, ask yourself: How do I already approach these? Can I tell the difference between them? Do I change the way I enter into a conversation or react based on the conversation type? If so, how? Let's explore the types of conversations you'll embark on with your child.

HEART–BASED CONVERSATIONS

Heart-based conversations are those that revolve around emotions and feelings. They include conversations about relationships, friendships, and intimacy. Heart-based conversations often feel like the hardest ones because so much rides on your relationship with your child. You have a vested interest in these conversations working out well because they provide the foundation for your own relationship and also for the relationships your child will have with others. Because conversations about matters of the heart are often delicate, parents can feel overwhelmed and unintentionally project their feelings of inadequacy or doubt.

The first intimate relationship your child will experience is with you, and it can be difficult to accept that others will follow. We may not like to imagine our children will ever need someone else the way they need us, and it is downright scary to know they will be hurt in some of their intimate relationships. The good news, though, is that when you engage in heart-based conversations you are preparing your child for happy and fulfilling relationships. Let your hope for their future guide you in teaching them how to trust and love.

All humans have emotions and, as adults, we are more practiced at recognizing them and controlling our behavior than kids are. That said, emotions affect you and the way you act. Try as you might to make sensible decisions, your brain cannot exclude the emotions you feel. The more aware of your emotions you are, the better you can control the way you express them. Just noting your feelings helps to trigger the rational thinking in your brain. Breathing deeply and retraining your thoughts can lower your heart rate and increase your ability to stay grounded during moments of emotional upheaval. It is important to understand how you deal with strong emotions, and we talk about subtypes of emotional expression in Chapter 5.

Then there's the issue of control, an everlasting dilemma for parents as children mature and naturally want more control over their lives. You can control yourself, for the most part, but you can't control others, and you must acknowledge what you bring to the conversation emotionally and what your child brings. Mitigate the issue of control by reading your child's body language and looking for cues and red flags. If your daughter appears frustrated (she rolls her eyes and gives one-word responses), she may benefit from taking control of the conversation, so take a back seat and see what she thinks. If that's not working, take a break and give her control by asking her to come to you when she's ready.

You can also relax your own body language, model deep breathing, and even do light yoga poses to help her enter a more relaxed state. Then help your child to name her emotions and find ways to work with them. Be mindful and empathetic. Empathy helps build relationships, and you can express empathy by being nonjudgmental and kind, and by offering help without strings attached. You can also show empathy through nonverbal language, like making soft eye contact as opposed to a stare-down, touching your child lightly, mirroring your child's body language, and exuding a relaxed, grounded mood. Think about absorbing your child's mood and feelings and gently reflecting them back before coming up with solutions or trying to a solve problem.

Consider the following situations and the opportunities they present for heart-based conversations. What might you do, say, or ask?

➤ Your daughter is distraught over a breakup.

➤ Your son no longer hangs around kids you know, and he seems to be a little different to you.

➤ A family member very close to you and your child has passed away.

➤ Your kids cannot stop bickering and it's driving you crazy; moreover, you worry that they will not have that long-lasting bond you hope for.

➤ Your daughter regularly refers to herself as stupid.

Read on in Chapter 5 to learn how to open heart-based conversations.

UNCOMFORTABLE CONVERSATIONS

Uncomfortable conversations are the ones that we know we should have but don't want to. They are about topics that feel awkward, including sex, diversity, or transitions. Uncomfortable conversations can be a challenge—for both you and your child—so acknowledge any discomfort up front. Signal to your child that, while you feel uncomfortable, this conversation is worth having. In addressing the awkward moments directly, you'll help to make those conversations more approachable. When your child sees you rise above the discomfort, he sees that these conversations mean something to you.

Have you ever felt flustered when someone cracked an inappropriate joke or made a comment about your appearance? How did you react? What did you do? Are you proud of your response? Why or why not? What might you do

A little flexibility can go a long way. Try doing some yoga to get everyone in the mood for flexible thinking. This activity can help ease a stressful moment and break the tension of a difficult conversation. Throw your legs up the wall and let your blood flow to your brain. Or strike a pose—a child's pose. Both of these positions are very relaxing, and they tease the body and mind into a state of relaxation.

Legs up the wall. This pose requires you to lay on your back with your bottom close to the wall and your legs up on the wall so that your legs are at a higher elevation than your heart. This is a great position for helping people calm down quickly and also for practicing meditation.

Child's pose. The child's pose is entered by sitting on your knees and folding your body on the ground so that your forehead is near the floor and your arms are out in front of you. You can stretch long, like a cat, to get the full effect. This pose is very relaxing and anxiety-reducing because you fold your body and relax all your tension into the ground. It may work best with a blanket beneath you; practice breathing calmly and evenly as your forehead moves down toward the floor.

Both legs up the wall and the child's pose are great for a quick break when things get heated and you need to recalibrate and de-stress.

differently? These are great stories to share with your child to teach him that such situations are difficult for anyone to navigate, even adults who have had a lot of experience with them. If, in hindsight, you felt you didn't respond in the way you would have liked, recognize your frustration—not only will this help you, it will teach your children to reflect on mistakes so they can make better, more informed decisions moving forward. Role-play scenes with your child to prepare for the next time something similar happens to either one of you and you want to respond differently. Address uncomfortable conversations head-on, and relate them back to real life when you can do so authentically.

Sharing your stories of discomfort and embarrassment, noting when you reacted well and when you didn't, offers a great model for your kid. This type of sharing is critical to developing vulnerability, and committing to these kinds of conversations—as uncomfortable as they may be—is a great way to show your kid how to have them. Sometimes we associate feelings of shame, frustration, or inadequacy with our discomfort, and digging into these feelings can help us to have the conversation rather than push those feelings down. These conversations are often the most difficult ones to have—and the most important, because so much pain can remain, fester, and create damage in these uncomfortable places.

Consider the following situations, and the opportunities they present for uncomfortable conversations. What might you do, say, or ask?

➤ You and your spouse are deciding whether to separate and you don't know what or how much to tell your kids, if anything.

➤ You suspect your son is having sex but you're not sure.

➤ You find pornography sites in the history of your daughter's computer.

➤ Your son just started wearing dresses and skirts to school.

➤ Your gut tells you something is wrong with your kid but you can't put your finger on it.

Read on in Chapter 6 to learn how to navigate uncomfortable conversations.

DANGEROUS CONVERSATIONS

Dangerous conversations are the ones you might wait to have because you think everything is okay—and then a situation comes on fast that forces you to face it head-on. Start dangerous conversations—mostly around safety, including drugs, alcohol, and assault—early so when it comes to this risky territory, the topics are not brand new. These conversations take precedence over all others simply because of the nature of the content. Ideally, you and your child have a strong foundation and have dangerous conversations before the threat is imminent, but no matter where you are in your relationship, jump in as soon as you observe a dangerous situation.

In these conversations, make it crystal clear that your child's health and safety are your foremost concerns, even above their happiness and your relationship. When it comes to priorities, the child's safety comes above all else.

Realize, though, that the more finger-wagging you do, the faster your child will retreat, so avoid blaming, threatening, and lecturing. When my friend's son came home from a sleepover and was vomiting all morning, my friend concluded he had been drinking. She was too angry to face him, and he was clearly not in a good state to talk between trips to the bathroom. When he came to dinner that evening he acted like everything was fine. After dinner, when they could talk in private, she asked him about the drinking. He was shocked—how did she know? She explained that she had made an educated guess, but, more importantly, if he hadn't been sick she might not have known, and they needed to talk about his choices. My friend was clear that she didn't want her son to drink, but she had never taken the time to talk with him about what happens if or when he does. This gave them the opportunity to talk about who he could call if he made the same decision and he didn't feel safe or if something went wrong.

When having dangerous conversations, make sure your expectations are clear. Did your child break a rule or lose your trust somehow? If you feel you were not clear or that your child acted inappropriately, talk through your concern or disappointment. Acknowledge your child's reasoning—while you may not agree with it, it played a role in his decision and, ultimately, you need to discuss how to handle future decision-making. If what your child has done warrants punishment, choose a consequence related to his lapse. Invite your child to help you come up with consequences rather than simply dictating punishment. Dangerous conversations should be a time for you to share your own worries and also a time for debate. These conversations will help to develop your child's judgment and decision-making.

Consider the following situations and the opportunities they present for dangerous conversations. What might you do, say, or ask?

➤ Your son comes to you with a secret and begs you to keep it quiet, but you think someone else should know.

➤ You find out your daughter has a profile on a dating website.

➤ You find a vaping JUUL in your son's pocket when you're doing laundry.

➤ You worry your daughter might be in an abusive relationship.

SETTING EXPECTATIONS

Set clear expectations for tweens and teens. Invite them to be a part of the process so they have ownership over the rules. Whenever you introduce a new milestone, like access to the car or a weekend at home without parents, talk about it ahead of time to be sure you both understand the concerns and to make some contingency plans. Ask your child if she has any ideas about how you can both feel safer.

Questions to ask might be: What are your plans for the weekend we'll be away? What do you think our expectations are about your behavior this weekend? We want you do be independent, but we worry. How can we set you up for success? (Here you may suggest check-ins over the weekend, a responsible neighbor to call, and a list of household responsibilities. These all create boundaries and help the teen to structure her weekend.)

➤ Your son has been driving for a year, and when you borrow his car you find empty beer bottles in the back seat.

Read on in Chapter 7 to learn how to brave dangerous conversations.

CHARACTER CONVERSATIONS

Character conversations are the ones that help you build your child's inner strength and help him to discover and define himself. They are the conversations about morals, values, and decision-making. Your job as a parent, after you've kept your child healthy and safe, is to raise a confident, happy, fulfilled, contributing member of society. No big deal, right?

How do we measure character? It's very difficult, considering that character shows in who your child is and how he behaves when you're not there giving him cues or instruction. When your child is very young, you are his primary model; as he grows, he is subject to many influences from the world around him. Your character conversations will help him learn to filter these outside influences and choose those that will serve him best as he becomes the person he wants to be.

As your child grows, the influencers in his life multiply. He will begin to notice what other kids do and think, and he will begin to care about that and to use the behavior of others as a guide. As you engage in character conversations with your tween or teen, know that what you have to say is still important—and, while your opinion may not be your child's sole influence, it's an important one.

Resist the urge to point out your child's character flaws; instead, talk about what you see that's working well and what you're proud of. Focus on the positive and point to examples. Set high expectations. When your child doesn't meet those, don't despair or assume he is a bad person. Good people make poor choices, and they simply need to reassess. Your child needs to know that he will make mistakes, but he can learn from those slip-ups to make better choices moving forward. Character conversations support your child's moral development, which will be crucial to making good decisions throughout his life. Work with him on the small missteps, like forgetting a homework assignment, so that you can build off that toward bigger decisions, such as whether to try marijuana.

Consider the following situations and the opportunities they present for character conversations. What might you do, say, or ask?

➤ Your son is failing a class and you find out at a parent-teacher conference.

➤ The principal of your daughter's school calls to tell you that there has been a breach of academic integrity.

➤ Your child seems to be making poor eating choices, and you're worried about her maintaining her energy levels and nutrition.

➤ Your son, all of a sudden (or so it seems), refuses to attend temple/ church/religious ceremonies with you.

➤ You don't like the way your daughter talks to you or you've seen some rude interactions between her and her friends online.

Read on in Chapter 8 to learn how to nurture character conversations.

BRAVE CONVERSATIONS

Brave conversations are ones that force us to go beyond our comfort zone to discuss something that might be scary or intimidating, such as bullying or struggling with confidence. We need to muster our courage because these conversations are sometimes hard to have, but they are essential; they also require us to model the courage we want to see in our children. For example, if you confronted unfairness at work and struggled to deal with it, share the experience to show your child how to speak up. When your child is in a similar situation, she will know there are options.

Let your child lead you into these conversations as much as you can, as courage may come more naturally to adolescents. They often see the intrinsic value in courage, as adolescence is all about self-discovery and exploration of the world.

Who better to understand and recognize bullying than a child in school? And who better to learn advocacy than that same child? So many of the situations adolescents face require them to be courageous, and it's unfair to expect them to handle situations if we don't prepare them with the right mindset. How can we expect tweens and teens to learn to take risks if we are constantly protecting them from failure? They will not learn to muddle their way through transitions if we smooth out all the hurdles.

Courage comes in all sizes, and it's important to celebrate appropriate risk-taking in matters both small and large. You provide the safety net through honest and forthright conversations—your child will know she can always depend on you, and that will give her the strength she needs. Courageous conversations help you and your child determine when it's right to take a risk and when your child isn't ready and needs to work up to her goal. They help provide context for your child the next time she needs to step up and advocate for herself or someone else.

Consider the following situations and the opportunities they present for brave conversations. What might you do, say, or ask?

➤ Your daughter has developed a lot of anxiety about going to school.

➤ Your son's confidence level appears to be at an all-time low.

➤ You see that your daughter has posted an inappropriate meme on social media directed at another kid at school.

➤ Your son wants to apply to a college you don't think you can afford.

➤ Your daughter's teacher recommends her for an honors course but she'd rather stay in her current courses so she can get better grades.

Read on in Chapter 9 to learn how to foster brave conversations.

Before we dive into the specific types of conversations—which make up Part 2—we'll teach you how to set the daily habit of talking with your kids and offer some answers to frequently asked questions.

"WE ARE WHAT WE REPEATEDLY DO. EXCELLENCE, THEN, IS NOT AN ACT BUT A HABIT."

WILL DURANT

Chapter 3

MAKING THE
PROJECT WORK

• • • • • • • • • • • •

"*W*hat is oral sex?" I remember asking this aloud when I was in elementary school to no one in particular as we sat down to dinner. In my memory, the topic had no stigma whatsoever. Dinner was the time and place to ask questions and for our family to interact. Family dinner was nonnegotiable, and most weeknights that meant eating at eight o'clock because that was the time we could all sit down together.

This was in the days before TiVo, and, while I was desperate to keep up with the primetime shows my friends were watching and would be discussing, I had something much more valuable: time with my family. Family dinner offered me the opportunity to hear about the day from everyone's perspective and to share my concerns and questions. Sometimes our conversations were about commonplace things in our lives, and sometimes we enjoyed (or didn't) intense arguments. But our relationships developed and traditions began.

The conversations we, as parents, have with our children today become the conversations we will have for life, and they are the foundation for our relationship. To make this project work, you need to build a habit of connecting with your kids every day. Habits are the building blocks of behavioral change. Assuming that you picked up this book to make a positive change in your relationship with your child, you will have to modify your own behavior in some ways and encourage your child to do the same. You likely already have some great habits in place you can build on: If you regularly drive your child to an activity, sit down together for a family meal, or watch a television show together, you are forming a foundation for relating to your child.

When planning a conversation, pick a topic from this book and begin asking questions and listening with intention to your child's responses. Be flexible. You may choose an activity to start the conversation or you may decide to focus on one of the prompts in Part 2 to get yourself off and running. It is natural that some days your efforts will lead to fruitful and affirming conversations, while on other days you will only draw out mundane daily content; and some days, a conversation may feel more like a chore than a pleasant exchange. Remember, you are building a habit of checking in and cultivating deeper discussions, and, as with any new habit, some days are easier than others.

HOW TO MAKE THE HABIT STICK

The key to making habits stick is consistency, repetition, and sequencing. Habits are formed in a three-step process. The first step is the cue, which triggers the brain to recognize the behavior that should follow. The second step is the routine—the actual behavior. And, finally, the third step is the reward. For example, if your favorite Friday TV show is on (cue) and you eat popcorn during this show every Friday (routine), then you may salivate when your TV show comes on, cueing you to make popcorn. The reward is the salty, crunchy snack. The habit is simply enjoying a television show every Friday with a bowl of popcorn. Fortunately for you, the conversation habit you're developing is one you'll want to continue for a lifetime. Stick with it and give it a chance.

As you and your child develop the habit of conversation, you will take control of your cues and routines. The critical habit is the conversation; the topics, seriousness, and settings can change as you face life's adventures and challenges. The important thing is to keep up the habit so that you learn to depend on it, and your child does, too.

Think about the times of day that offer the best opportunities for talking, and make sure they suit both you and your child. You may be more open after dinner, for example, because you're not thinking about work, but your child might be preoccupied with homework then. Identify a few alternatives and try

Family dinner is a great place to start your new conversation habit. Over the past few decades, the number of weekly meals families share together has decreased. And when families do eat together, the time is often filled with distractions such as television or cell phones. If you can make shared meals a regular habit, consider it. Family meals are shown to be a protective factor for kids, offering them a place to be connected to their family (i.e., not connected to their phones). Research suggests that setting aside regular time to spend with your kids leads to better communication and kids who engage in fewer risky behaviors.

them out. Remember, you have to create the routine until the reward automatically kicks in and forms the habit.

Once you have noticed that a certain time lends itself to conversation, think about what cue or trigger you want to choose. Cues to consider include brewing tea, making popcorn, lighting a candle, sitting down for a cuddle, grabbing this book, or getting two glasses of water.

Give your kid some say in the cue, space, and time you choose. He might really look forward to ginger beer and crackers and a soft blanket, or he might want tea with cookies as he sprawls on the floor. Decide together which situation will be most enjoyable, and your daily check-ins will become a habit that you both look forward to. If you've taken care to ensure that it's a two-way conversation—with topics and routines your child has helped choose—he will help keep the tradition going.

For the sake of consistency, choose the same space and same time to talk every day, at least as you are forming the habit. If consistency is difficult due to your schedule, try to make sure you're finding time each day, even if the time slot itself changes. Rather than stressing about it, find a makeup time or extend your next conversation.

SETTING A GOOD HABIT

We often look for ways to break bad habits, but here you'll focus on creating a new, productive, and engaging habit: talking with your kids about the things that matter most. Choose the three steps that will help you establish a strong conversation habit:

1. A trigger to spark the behavior.

2. A routine to practice the behavior.

3. A reward to celebrate the behavior.

Pay attention and savor the reward of closeness and connection. Enjoy the warm, secure feeling that comes from creating a bond with your kid. If you have more than one child, consider how combining check-ins and talking with two or more kids at once will change the conversation, as well as when that tactic is and is not appropriate.

And just because you have a special time of day to talk does not mean you can't engage in meaningful conversations at other times. In fact, this daily habit of checking in will encourage productive conversations all day.

CRACKING THE CONVERSATION CODE: USING YOUR "F" WORDS

Here are three "F" words that will keep the conversation going: flexibility, fluidity, and flow. These three words relate closely to one another and help out when you're searching for a way to keep the conversation rolling. Remind yourself, and your child, to use your "F" words.

"Flexibility" refers to a willingness to move—from topic to topic, from setting to setting, or from tone to tone. Even if you strike up the conversation, be willing to take your child's lead if she seems to be going in a new direction. And if she appears to be changing direction because she feels uncomfortable, bring up that uneasiness. You might both feel awkward but being open to her words and acknowledging the uncomfortable feelings can help to break the ice. Push forward and try to have the conversation, even if the going is a little bumpy.

"Fluidity" is a sense of back-and-forth. Conversations are a two-way street (even a multilane freeway, at times). Make sure you allow your child to be a full participant in the conversation, in terms of content and time. Be a good participant by sharing and listening.

"Flow" suggests you go where the current takes you. Whatever comes up, go with it and make the most of it. Allow for true conversations; while you may control the timing and setting to some degree, don't control the actual conversation—otherwise, it becomes a monologue or a lecture.

It is very important to "go with the flow" when embarking on this project. There is no right or wrong way to have conversations with your kids. While this book offers a template for jump-starting conversations, tailor the conversations to your own family's dynamic and values. Pay attention to your kid, and judge when she has had enough talking or wants to switch to a different subject. This doesn't necessarily mean switching the subject when things get uncomfortable, because this sticky place fosters growth. But you should pay attention and listen and look carefully at your kid when speaking with her rather than trying to get through an agenda. If you stay flexible and fluid, and go with the flow, you will be able to engage authentically with your child and embrace the project fully.

LEARN SOMETHING NEW ABOUT YOUR KID AND YOURSELF

I remember playing a board game called Loaded Questions with my husband and kids. We enjoyed some laughs, but more importantly I learned something about my kids that day. The game asks all the players to answer the same question and the person whose turn it is has to guess which response matches which player. The first time we played, my daughter answered the question, "What was the most exciting day of your life?" with, "The day we dug the hole."

SHUTTING DOWN

"I am not talking right now. Leave me alone." You may experience this shutdown from your tween/teen. This behavior can mean many different things. It may be he simply had a busy day, is frustrated with homework, or had a misunderstanding with a friend. In many cases, it could be an emotional overload and he may just need an emotional "time out." This should be respected and allowed. If your child seems to want to be with you, consider spending your time together another way—take a walk, cook dinner, or watch TV to "ride out the storm." Later, set aside a time to sit together, maybe with tea or a sweet treat, and open the conversation up again. Tips to restarting the conversation include:

Be patient. Sit and be together. Don't rush the conversation.

Ask questions. Avoid talking at your child; ask for his opinion.

Be quiet. Certainly feel free to share, but don't fill the air with talk for the sake of talking.

Don't be anxious. Getting upset and shutting down is part of the process for your child, so know that and be okay with the quiet and the awkwardness.

Relate. Share your own stories about being uncomfortable, and maybe include some of your own coping strategies. Ask if your child has any to suggest to you.

Be honest. Tell him how you feel in this moment and what, ideally, you would like to have happen.

Create a "no judgment" zone. Be very clear that you are open to anything being said and will reserve judgment in return.

It is important for you to return to the conversation—it signals to your child that you are paying attention to all aspects of his life and that you are not afraid of speaking about tough subjects. The tough stuff is where we are tested and where the real connection and bond is formed, so dig in and open up the conversation as many times as you must.

I remember sitting back and thinking, "What day was that, and what made it so interesting?" My daughter's answer spurred a conversation about an event that had occurred during recess with her friends. I knew nothing about it until that conversation. Teaming with your child, you will learn more about each other and yourselves through your daily check-ins. For this process to be truly productive and transformative, both of you have to be fully invested and willing to dive in deep. This can occasionally feel uncomfortable or frustrating, but over time, the relationship will build and questions will come more organically.

As you embark on this new adventure, demonstrate self-empathy and be kind to yourself. Consider how you talk to and about yourself. Are you generous in your self-descriptions? Do you paint yourself in the way you'd like your kids to see you? Is there anything you'd like to change about the way you talk to yourself? What would that sound like? Can you write a script that shows how you want to talk to yourself or about yourself differently? What corresponding behaviors would support this new type of self-talk? For example, if you say to yourself, "It's okay to not be perfect all the time; I value my ability to bounce back from mistakes..." what do you need to do to walk the talk? Corresponding behaviors could include taking risks, getting support from family and friends, journaling about your feelings, setting goals about branching out and trying new things, or embracing your imperfections.

COMMON CONCERNS

Many parents have concerns regarding conversation and confrontation with their kids, including getting kids to really listen, sustaining eye contact, overcoming their own discomfort, and wondering how effective the conversation is.

Often, when we have concerns or when something is wrong, we have an urge to jump in and fix it. Much conversation is about working through challenges and finding solutions. Part of your job as a parent is to offer your child skills and strategies that will help him help himself. In teaching your child how to talk with you, you are teaching him how to talk with others and how to build trusting and productive relationships. In essence, you are teaching your child to be his own person and to ignite his own conversations in the same way you are starting them with him.

Conversation need not be confrontational. In fact, the environment should be set so that the conversation is reciprocal, comfortable, and open. It is true that the best conversations happen organically, but, given how busy we all are, it is best to scaffold a conversation and pick a time and place to talk with your kids.

"HOW DO I GET MY KID TO REALLY LISTEN?"

Many parents don't think their kids hear them, but kids are listening. And, believe it or not, constant repetition and nagging is not the magical answer to getting your child's attention. For the most part, kids want to please their parents and rise to expectations. If you focus on what's important and instill the core message over time rather than constantly nagging, your kids will hear you. Also, remember that messaging can be nonverbal, so modeling your expectations and offering support can be very effective.

"WHAT IF MY KID DOESN'T AGREE WITH ME?"

Hearing you does not mean your child agrees with you. In fact, when your child disagrees she is actually demonstrating her independence and willful mind. This is a good thing. You want your kid to hear you, to process your points, and to synthesize her own conclusion, not yours. Granted, your child's opinions are not refined, so following her own conclusions will likely lead to some poor choices and mistakes. But that's how you learned and that's how your kids learn, too. We need to falter to understand what success is.

"HOW DO I GET MY KID TO LOOK ME IN THE EYE WHEN WE TALK?"

It is a great idea to practice making eye contact in conversations with your child. Good eye contact will serve your child in conversations and also when he needs to have that serious talk with a teacher, a friend, or even a colleague down the line. Let your child know when eye contact is necessary. Sometimes, a friendly request is all it takes: "Please look at me while we're talking." And sometimes establishing appropriate eye contact will require more practice and reminders. Avoid admonishing kids when they look away. Be a model and be patient. Kids may refrain from looking at you when they are nervous, scared, or ashamed. Reassure them that you're both in this conversation and they can trust you.

Keep in mind that some conversations are actually more effective without eye contact. If you're struggling to connect, or if one (or both) of you feels awkward, it can help to have the conversation while you're doing an activity or riding in the car. Choose carefully, so you instill the importance of eye contact when appropriate but aren't always demanding it.

"HOW DO I OVERCOME MY OWN DISCOMFORT WITH DIFFICULT TOPICS IN ORDER TO TALK WITH MY KID ABOUT THEM?"

Ideally, with enough conversation and practice, you will become comfortable with even the most difficult subjects—or at least you'll get *more* comfortable. That said, you don't have to wait to be comfortable to have the conversation. In fact, acknowledging your discomfort shows your child two things: 1) it's important to have a conversation even if you are uncomfortable, and 2) you care enough about your child to step out of your comfort zone and help him through this important topic. So, for starters, tell your child up front that you're not comfortable and why, and then jump in. If he asks questions you cannot answer, make sure you look up the answers and get back to him.

"WHAT IF MY KID IS DISTRACTED OR DISINTERESTED?"

It can be difficult to tell if a child is distracted or simply not engaged in the way we expect her to be. It's normal for a kid to want to be out of the conversation, especially when the conversation is serious, so try your best to be patient and understanding. Often, lack of eye contact can signal disinterest or discomfort. But if a child is actively doing something else, like having a separate conversation either in person or via a mobile device, it's pretty clear she is distracted.

Take a moment to think about how you entered the conversation and if you've chosen an optimal time for it. Sometimes we don't have the luxury of waiting, but if you do, find a time when you can both put everything down and truly talk. If you've identified a good time and your child is still preoccupied, try not to take it personally. Find out why she is distracted, and, if possible, give her space to take care of what she needs to do. Then ask for her complete attention. Technology can be a huge distraction, but it can also be a connector, so try to embrace it for what it is and use it to your advantage when you can.

"WHAT IF MY CHILD REFUSES TO PARTICIPATE IN THE CONVERSATION?"

A conversation with an unresponsive child can be frustrating, but try to think of it as part of the process. It's normal for your child to stay quiet, and that's okay. Say what you need to say and provide time and space for your child to respond. It can feel like forever when you're waiting for someone to respond and he doesn't, but give it time and patience. Sit quietly together and wait. If, after a few minutes, your child doesn't say anything, ask if he wants to respond and whether he needs more time.

If you're really stumped, take a break. When you try to engage again, start with a casual entry into the conversation. Plan a conversation starter in your mind and be ready to walk it back, if necessary, until you're both ready to talk. If the subject is urgent, try writing a letter, an email, or even a text to get the conversation started. It's best to continue the conversation in person if it's important, but at least you can get things going.

"HOW DO I KNOW IF I NEED TO TALK TO MY KID URGENTLY?"

If something in your child's behavior sets off alarms and you're not sure whether to step in quickly or to tread carefully, err on the side of quickly. Your gut might be telling you something. Red flags include your child's behavior changed; your child seems moodier than usual; she seems to be hanging with different friends; her diet or sleeping habits have changed. These could all be normal, part of growing up, but they could also signal a more significant change.

If you are at all worried that your child will hurt herself or someone else, stop everything and ask for external help. Good resources to lean on include your child's teachers, a school counselor or psychologist, or your child's pediatrician. And, if those resources are not the right ones, they will often have good referrals for you. It's okay to feel that a problem is too much for you to handle on your own, no matter your professional and personal experience.

If your child's behavior is not particularly worrying and your intuition tells you that her troubles are of a more mundane variety, you can take a slower course. As parents, we often want to step in immediately when we sense something is wrong. It's great if you can have an authentic conversation right away but it's not always necessary, so don't panic if you want to take a moment to process what's going on. It is often better to have a good conversation after you've had time to think than a quick conversation where you might say things you didn't mean.

"HOW DO I KNOW IF THIS CONVERSATION IS HELPING OR HURTING MATTERS?"

You may find yourself wondering, "Is this conversation worth having?" The answer is almost always yes. The better question might be, "Am I starting this conversation in an appropriate way?" or, "Am I the right person for my child to be talking to right now?"

If you are worried or are curious about anything going on in your child's life, it's worth talking with him. You may not know right off the bat if the conversation is helping, but you can look for signs that tell you he isn't ready to hear you or confide in you. These include your child refusing to make eye contact, being unresponsive or rude, being distracted, or arguing with you.

If you determine that your attempt at the conversation is not helping, but you know it's an important one to have, encourage your child to talk with someone you trust. Together with your child, identify a person who would be a good resource, perhaps an aunt, an uncle, a guidance counselor, a close family friend, or a coach. Make sure you have talked with the person and that you trust his judgment and he is prepared to guide your child in a way that is consistent with your family's values.

"WHAT IF THE CONVERSATION BECOMES CONFRONTATIONAL?"

It's okay if your conversations sometimes become confrontational. Disagreement is not something to avoid, but you should handle it in a productive way, which can be difficult when emotions run high. Confrontation can feel awkward and push us to say or do things we later regret. Try to understand, as best you can, where your child is coming from and meet her there. You'll be surprised what a few breaths can do for you in the moment. And if the confrontation feels overwhelming, take a time out and get back into the conversation when you are

WHEN SHUTTING DOWN IS DANGEROUS

Some situations require special attention. If your child talks about hurting another person or himself, you need to act immediately. You must talk with your teen about how seriously he thinks about hurting himself or others, if he has a specific plan, and if he has access to weapons or drugs. If you are concerned about your child not being safe, take him to the nearest emergency room for a psychological assessment. If you are concerned about the safety of your child and he won't get into the car, call 911.

calmer. Remember, you are teaching your child how to behave in difficult situations, so you should convey that you are not afraid of confrontation but that sometimes it's a good idea to step back for a little while.

"WHAT IF I'M IN OVER MY HEAD?"

On occasion, it's better to refrain from conversations with your child. Times like these might include when you believe your child is considering harming himself or others, if you feel your child has sunk into a deep depression, or if you suspect he has a substance abuse issue. In these situations, be sure your child is talking with a trusted adult or, if appropriate, a professional who can help him, and let him know you are there for him no matter what. While you can certainly talk with your child about the problem, it is likely bigger than you, so make sure you have the appropriate supports in place for yourself and your child.

"SHOULD ALL CONVERSATIONS BE ONE-ON-ONE?"

The idea behind building a habit of conversation is to develop a relationship with your child. While many conversations can include the whole family and still achieve this goal, some conversations are best one-on-one. For example, if you want to discuss something personal, like a boyfriend, a failing grade, or perhaps something regarding punishment, consider having it one-on-one. Depending on the conversation, two adults talking to one child can feel confrontational. If one adult talks with multiple kids at the same time, the kids won't get the individual attention and privacy they need for deep-level conversations.

Next, we'll consider conversation as a process and show you how to get started as well as how to modify your verbal and nonverbal behavior to foster the kind of connection you want.

"LISTENING IS MUCH MORE THAN ALLOWING ANOTHER TO TALK WHILE WAITING FOR A CHANCE TO RESPOND. . .THE BEAUTY OF LISTENING IS THAT THOSE WHO ARE LISTENED TO START FEELING ACCEPTED, START TAKING THEIR WORDS MORE SERIOUSLY AND DISCOVERING THEIR OWN TRUE SELVES. LISTENING IS A FORM OF SPIRITUAL HOSPITALITY BY WHICH YOU INVITE STRANGERS TO BECOME FRIENDS."

HENRI NOUWEN

Chapter 4

CONVERSATION STARTERS
AND STRATEGIES

• • • • • • • • • • • • •

When I was eighteen years old, I invited a strange man into my car. I was driving a friend home on a rainy night and saw a man on the side of the road with what appeared to be a broken-down car. I felt badly for him and stopped to see if I could make a call. This was before cell phones, and I offered to make the call from my friend's house. He asked if I could just give him a lift to his daughter's house. I didn't want to appear rude, so I let him in the car. I knew in my gut that I was making a mistake, and yet I gave him a ride. It all turned out okay; he truly just needed to get to his daughter's house. I've replayed that scene in my head many times, knowing that it could have ended very differently.

When I've shared that story with my kids, I've been open that I probably made a dumb choice. My gut was telling me to get out of the situation. While things worked out fine, I took an ill-advised chance with my safety. What can I learn from the experience? What different choices could I make moving forward so I would feel more in control? Is offering strangers a ride ever okay? By sharing that I don't necessarily have all the answers, I signal to my kids that we all make mistakes and can learn from them, and that I am open to my kids' ideas and mistakes.

As parents, we often swing between wanting to encourage our children to be independent and wanting to shield them from the world. But there is a way to balance these competing desires, to provide realistic guidance and advice in a direct and deliberate way. Conversation is your tool to share your ideas and set expectations for behavior. Be clear that your role is to keep your child safe, but also to teach your child to be her own person. It takes years to develop as a person, so the key is to provide opportunities for your child to demonstrate independence. Then talk about the choices your child makes. These opportunities give kids the chance to earn your trust and provide subject matter for your conversations. Take the time to talk through decisions your child has made rather than assuming your child knows right from wrong.

When talking with your children, don't force the outcome of the conversation; understand that the conversation should be ongoing and flexible. Many of the topics we suggest are provocative and may be tough to bring up. Start with a topic that feels easier and work up to the harder conversations. Alternatively, consider simply telling your child that this is tough for you and then forge ahead. You will likely need to return to the same conversations again and again, especially the prickly ones, so be sure to let your kids know that no single conversation on a topic is enough. Also let them know that they should feel free to come up with their own questions and information to share with you.

CREATING CONVERSATIONS FOR LIFE

The conversations you begin with your child now will help you continue those conversations for life. The more open you are with each other and the more trust you develop, the stronger your relationship will be. Make sure your child knows you are there, no matter what, even if you don't have all the answers.

SOLICIT TOPIC IDEAS

While you as the parent will have to act as the role model and initiate some of the big ideas, you and your child should decide together where the conversation goes; it's not a one-way street. Consider ways to solicit topics from your child if she doesn't naturally bring them up. Use a journal or create a box to collect different topics or ideas during the week. This could make for some fun dinner banter (especially when your kid's friends are over). Invite your child's questions and don't shy away from the hard ones. If you don't know the answer to a question, research the topic together.

CHANGE THE TONE

Changing your tone of voice can have a tremendous effect on behavior. By softening your voice, you will lower stress in both yourself and your child, leading to a positive result.

The next time you feel the need to raise your voice, try whispering to your child and notice how her behavior changes immediately. Have you asked your child to feed the dog, pick up a towel, or get her shoes on twenty-five times? Instead of saying it the twenty-sixth time, whisper the request playfully in your child's ear. Notice her reaction—it may be a smile, a laugh, or a whisper back. This technique utilizes the element of surprise, which will be sure to get your child's attention.

KEEP THE CONVERSATION GOING

Keep communication open and ongoing. If it's hard to generate conversations and your kids aren't offering much, consider putting up a large whiteboard where family members can write questions and comments. Divide the board into categories; these can be about television programs or things that happen at school—anything! Then find a time to get together to address all the questions and comments. This allows people to think about the questions they ask and creates time to process responses. It also encourages the ongoing communication that doesn't always come naturally to developing tweens and teens.

GETTING STARTED

The following tips will help you plan a conversation and also evaluate how a conversation is going or how it went. Use your best judgment and find the right time, tone, and place to talk. And if the conversation doesn't go well or needs to be expanded, consider what parts of it should remain the same in the future and what needs to be altered. Use the Conversation Checklist as a quick guide or refresher to keep yourself on track.

CONVERSATION CHECKLIST

TONE

- Have you struck the right tone?

- Are you comfortable and does your child appear to be comfortable or is there tension?

- Is your child offering one-word answers or avoiding eye contact?

- Does she seem to be angry or frustrated?

- If you haven't hit the right tone, how can you alter it?

SETTING

- Is the space for your conversation comfortable for both you and your child?

- Is the level of distraction appropriate and helpful, or are you losing focus?

- If you are not in the right physical space, find a more suitable spot or take a rain check.

TIMING

- Is this an optimal time for the conversation?

- If not, can it be postponed?

NONVERBAL INTERACTION

- Does your body language convey trust, openness, and honesty, with open body posture, gentle eye contact, a smile, and head nods?

- Are you subtly mirroring your child's nonverbal behavior?

- Be thoughtful about the way you listen and talk. Your child pays attention to all you say with your words *and* your body.

TONE

Consider your intentions as you jump into the conversation. Is the conversation serious? Is it important for you to remain calm? Are you trying to infuse excitement? Tone of voice is a therapist's best instrument. Therapists learn how to modify their voices to express different emotions and provide a client with comfort and safety.

Parents can learn to use this trusted tool as well. If your child is anxious, try whispering, slowing down your voice, and speaking with intention. If your child is timid, use your voice to sound excited and enthusiastic. At times, it helps to mimic the tone, nonverbal actions, and behavior of your child. This signals to your child that he is "heard" or understood—a very important piece in building a foundation of trust.

If the conversation isn't going quite right, try simply saying something like, "I think we got off on the wrong foot. Can we reset?" Or you may need to step back and revisit the conversation later when you or your child can manage a better tone.

SETTING

When choosing a setting for a conversation, think about whether it will be important to make eye contact and consider the distractions that might be helpful or harmful. Sometimes you don't have a lot of choice in the matter; if that's the case, make the best of the situation by focusing and making time for the conversation. Have the confidence to change location if needed, or, if that is not possible, know that you can push pause on the conversation until you can find a more appropriate spot.

If something you need to talk about is erupting right now and right here, and there is no way to move the conversation or put it on hold, take a deep breath and forge ahead, but consider how the location might affect what you say and do.

Here are some good ways to manage the setting to make your conversations more comfortable:

➤ **Take a drive.** The car is a great place to have a conversation if eye contact isn't crucial. A drive can also be calming if music is playing and no one else is around to distract. You often have a captive audience when you're ferrying your child to an activity. Of course, you need to be focused on safe driving; pull over if you get too deep into the conversation to focus on your driving.

PLEASE PUT THE PHONE DOWN!

Is it okay, when having a conversation, if your phone stays near you but turned off, turned upside down, or whatever? Unfortunately, the answer is no. Hence, the "iPhone effect," famously coined in a 2014 University of Virginia study by psychologist Shalini Misra. Researchers observed one hundred couples in a coffee shop and found that, even if the phone was off, the presence of the phone on the table had a negative effect on the conversation. In essence, people were less likely to talk about significant feelings and were less empathic.

If your child is distracted by his phone, allow him time to have that connection to his world before forcing him out of it. For example, when you pick your kid up from school, allow him a few minutes to decompress and check his phone before demanding his attention. But then, do expect that he'll pay attention.

➤ **Go for a walk.** You'll have some privacy and a change of scenery. The fresh air and natural surroundings will help calm you and your child. And exercise is good if the conversation gets emotional.

➤ **Take it to the child's room.** Kids like to talk in their rooms, often around bedtime. This allows them to stay up a little later, and they might let some of their defenses down as they're unwinding from the day. The child's room can be a great place to have private, sensitive conversations about topics such as sex, bullying, or love.

➤ **Shop and talk.** Shopping can be a fun outing for both you and your child—there's a reason it's called retail therapy! Don't embark on a big conversation when you're shopping for just the right prom outfit or a prized gift, however. Try talking during a routine grocery shop or maybe a fun outing for clothes or books. Shopping for trivial items is good when you want to talk about topics that are likely to lead to lots of questions or that need some time to ponder and digest.

➤ **Take a break.** Vacations offer you a different environment, which opens up new perspectives and ideas. You are also less concerned with your day-to-day obligations.

➤ **Grab a bite.** Going out to dinner or for ice cream can alter the scene while still allowing for dedicated family time. Also, consider taking your child out for a meal one-on-one, to create a special evening and provide some more get-to-know-you time.

➤ **Multitask.** You want your child to know he is the center of your focus when you're talking about something important. That said, a slight distraction can sometimes be handy—making dinner together, working on a household project, or cleaning up allows you to share in a chore, work on something worthwhile, and talk in a natural way. Sometimes, having your hands busy is good for the brain and can make conversations feel less imposing. If you're engaged in a project, you are not overly focused on the conversation and have the project to fall back on should the conversation get very intense. It also provides a casual atmosphere, demonstrating to your child that conversation is welcome at any time.

TIMING

If you can, time your conversation appropriately for your child. Is she a morning person? Or does she like to push bedtime as late as possible? If she's a night owl, starting a conversation at bedtime may encourage her to participate more. Timing a conversation can be tricky, and you want to find a time when you can explore a topic fully without schedule constraints. Often, though, we don't have the luxury of time and need to make fast decisions. Realize that it's never too late to revisit a conversation to share more or ask questions you wished you had asked.

First thing in the morning can be an ideal time for emotional temperature taking or cheerleading a new skill or idea. For example, if you spoke with your child the night before about friendships and together came up with a game plan for addressing a sticky friendship issue, a quick recap and reminder would be fitting in the morning. Generally speaking, one of the best times to talk is after dinner and homework are finished, as the brain starts to rest and kids are more able to relax and talk about personal topics.

NONVERBAL INTERACTION

The majority of our communication is nonverbal, consisting of eye contact, facial gestures, hand gestures, and body posture. Learning to moderate your nonverbal behavior when talking with your children is paramount in creating an atmosphere of trust, openness, and honesty. As a warm, authoritative parent, you can display these qualities with an open body posture. This means literally being physically open—keep your hands at your side; turn fully toward your child; maintain direct, gentle eye contact; have a soft smile; and use slight head nods in response to what your child is saying. With this type of body language, you are letting your child know she is important and you are paying attention to her—you are in this with her.

Think of a mother talking with her son about drinking and drugs. She starts the conversation with her hands on her hips, a stern look on her face, and an

FAKE IT 'TIL YOU MAKE IT

Are you having problems dealing with confrontation and frustration from your child? Do as the popular aphorism says, and fake it 'til you make it. Did you know that when you smile, even if you force it, your body secretes the famous "happiness chemicals" serotonin and dopamine? In addition, your physical posture and hand gestures signal in a feedback loop to your brain, helping to dictate the tone of your communication. Even if you are not in the best of moods, you can "fake" positive nonverbal communication, and the good feelings will follow. Smiling, laughing, and hugging are all nonverbal exercises that can build a more positive state of mind. Try this technique yourself, and then share it with your child.

intense eye gaze. She says to her son, "You know, Johnny, I would love for you to come talk with me about drinking and drugs. I want you to be completely comfortable with me so that we can talk openly." Unfortunately, this mother's words will only go so far because her nonverbal cues indicate a rigid and possibly confrontational stance. An open-body posture will tell her son that she is truly ready to hear him.

Neuroscientific research has advanced our understanding of human emotions and provided us with useful information for becoming great communicators. The limbic brain includes the amygdala, hippocampus, cingulated gyrus, orbital frontal cortex, and insula. The amygdala is considered the "emotional center" of the brain, and it investigates all information coming into consciousness. This emotional center becomes stimulated very quickly when situations are either physically or psychologically threatening. The limbic brain quickly deciphers nonverbal information—body language, tone of voice, pheromones, and eye contact—in order to help make sense of all information.

How important is nonverbal communication? Many neuroscientists would say that it does not matter what you say, but *how* you say it. That is, research shows that when people display nonverbal gestures (such as a cold, closed posture) that are contradictory to their verbal communication (a giggling, bubbly conversational style), people will disregard that person because the message does not make sense. In Malcom Gladwell's book *Blink*, he cites examples of behavior combined with the fast and furious judgments people make about those behaviors. So, for better or worse, the more you know about communicating clearly in nonverbal ways, the more effective you will be as a parent.

Another technique famously utilized by therapists is the "mirroring technique." This technique involves simply following the lead of the person you are talking to. For example, if your child talks while tilting her head to the left, then you tilt your head as well; when she smiles, you smile back. This technique is best when done subtly—don't overdo it. The goal is to help your child understand that you are empathizing with her. She will also learn to pick up on this behavior, and you might notice her mirroring you—this teaches social grace. Note that teenagers can get annoyed if this mirroring technique is heavy-handed, as it may appear that you are mocking them.

Once you have adjusted your nonverbal language to denote openness and empathy, it is time to decipher your child's nonverbal language. My ten-year-old son, for example, pulls on his neck when he is nervous. When I notice this behavior, I ask him, "Is everything okay? Is there anything I do to help?" Your child has ways of communicating with you without using spoken language, and once you know how to translate you will be better able to deal with confrontations, help with tender emotions, and quell anxiety. Adjusting your body language, and reading your child's, allows you to become more confident and less anxious, and will help you both connect more.

Now you've got the tone, setting, timing, and nonverbal cues down, you will be surprised by how quickly your child follows your lead into the conversation.

GETTING THE DISENGAGED KID ON BOARD

If you've read up to this point and you think your kid still won't participate, that he'll stay silent, here are some ideas to try:

- ➤ **Be direct.** Let your kid know that you're trying, and you want some two-way communication.

- ➤ **Make contact.** Put a hand on your child's shoulder, make eye contact, or give a hug, and then ask, "What would you like to do?" Physical touch releases oxytocin, which naturally reduces stress in our bodies.

- ➤ **Take a break.** If it's not happening, don't force it. You tried, and the message is getting across, even if slowly. Come back in a bit and let your kid know this conversation will happen, no matter how long it takes, and that you will be as patient as you can.

- ➤ **Change the environment.** Go for a walk or sit on the couch. See if it helps to be in a new, more relaxing place.

- ➤ **Put a pin in it.** Sometimes saying nothing is better than saying something. If the conversation is not flowing, then hold off—for now.

- ➤ **Ask your child.** Ask, "What is going on?" Find out if your kid has an idea about why it's so hard to talk. Give your kid choices. For example, "Would you prefer to continue talking now or tomorrow?" State the importance of conversation but don't rush the process.

STRATEGIES

Some general strategies will help you engage in conversations with kids, making sure your participation is productive. In Part 2 we offer specific activities and prompts for different types of conversation. When you try them out, keep the following in mind:

- ➤ **Focus on the positive.** It's easy to fixate on what's not going well or on a stumbling block. Instead, enter the conversation with an open mind and don't place blame or point out the challenges. If your child's behavior is the reason for the conversation, start and end on a positive note about something he does that you admire or enjoy.

➤ **Maintain an open dialogue.** Remember, this is not the first or last time you and your child will talk, and it may not even be the first or last time you will talk about the topic at hand. Make sure your child knows any topic is fair game and any question is legitimate.

➤ **Reserve judgment.** It is natural to judge, and we often do it before we can stop ourselves. Do your best to refrain from sharing your opinion until you have had a chance to process the situation. Think about what you hear and be careful not to overreact.

➤ **Stay calm.** Many of the conversations we have with our children get us excited, and not always in a positive way. Try to keep your cool. It's okay if your child sees you falter, search for words, or take a breath.

➤ **Listen, don't fix.** Being there for your child is more important than making sure everything is right. Your child won't learn how to problem solve if you don't allow her the space to do it herself.

➤ **Validate your child's feelings and concerns.** You don't have to validate your child's actions or behavior, but you should acknowledge where he's coming from and his perspective. Let him know that you understand (or are trying to understand) his feelings and that it's okay to feel as he does.

➤ **Identify a safe person.** Of course, you're having ongoing conversations to develop your relationship with your child, and hopefully your child will know you want her to come to you with any problems or concerns. But let her know it's okay if she isn't comfortable talking to you about certain things. Identify a person (or two) that you are comfortable with her going to, and make sure your child has the person's contact info. Also be sure the go-to person knows his role.

➤ **Jump in.** If the opportunity for a conversation arises, don't be afraid to jump in, even if you feel underprepared. Trust your gut and proceed with care.

- **Be direct.** As the saying goes, honesty is the best policy. When you waffle, your child will pick up on your indecision and uncertainty. This doesn't mean you always need to have the answer, but you should be clear in your decision-making. If you change your mind, be clear about that.

- **Ask open-ended questions.** Explore questions that don't have definite answers—and be prepared that your child may respond with something you aren't expecting. This is when reserving judgment or pausing can help you regain your equilibrium and frame a productive reply.

- **Practice role-playing.** Role-playing can be a fascinating way to practice appropriate conversations, and it's also a great way to get to know each other. If your child is struggling with a relationship with a friend or teacher, role-play a conversation. This allows your child to practice what she might say and builds some comfort as she prepares to face that friend or teacher.

- **Tell stories.** Use personal stories to exemplify your point. This is a great way for your child to get to know you better and for you to share experiences without it coming off as a lecture.

- **Listen mindfully.** When you listen, truly tune in to what your child says. This doesn't mean you should be passive; rather, you must be active without talking. Reflect on what your child says, restate her words to be certain you understand, and refrain from judging, signaling that you hear her and value her opinion.

- **Let go of expectations.** Be ready for what comes. This means being open for a true two-way conversation. When you have expectations, you set yourself up for disappointment, and your kids can see that.

- **Check your emotional temperature.** Consider your feelings as you talk with your child. Assigning a number value to your emotions helps you self-assess and also provides a descriptor you can share with your child if you like: 5 is feeling great, 4 is doing well, 3 is feeling okay, 2 is feeling not so good, and 1 is feeling terrible. It's good to check your child's emotional temperature throughout the conversation, as well. If your child is a visual learner, use a visual aid to illustrate the temperature gauge.

➤ **Incorporate memories.** Talk about fun times that brought you together. Remember silly or embarrassing things that will spark a reaction. This helps you establish a joyful moment and build trust.

➤ **Identify feelings.** Help your child name what she feels. When your child was a toddler she made demands, and when she didn't have the right words or you didn't understand, she would grow frustrated and maybe even throw a fit. Tweens and teens feel similar frustration. They have budding feelings and hormones surging unevenly in their bodies, and they often express their frustration through stubborn or rude behavior. Kids need to learn what is causing their frustration so they can understand themselves better and gain more control over their behavior.

CONVERSATION AS A PROCESS

Conversation is a process, and in this chapter we've looked at many ways to begin that process. Now you have to keep the conversation going. Think about the progress of your conversations, and note whether they are getting richer in substance. It is important to praise progress and development over time, taking into account a growth mindset. Believing that we can grow and change and do not have personalities that are fixed or inflexible is important for this project. People start from different places and will want to end up in the different places, and that is okay. Focus on progress and the increasing depth of your conversations rather than on the length of conversations or completion of all the exercises in the book. The goal is growth.

Celebrate any openness or reciprocated conversation. Really lean into it. Remember that participation is better than disengagement, even if participation means silent listening. Kids talk and relate differently—they are different from one another and from adults—so be patient and take the time to learn about your own communication style and that of your child. Even little behavior differences can throw us off. If we want our children to learn how to accept themselves, we must accept them for who they are. And this acceptance, in turn, will teach them to accept us for who we are.

Allow yourself to listen. Try not to formulate responses while others are talking, and let yourself process what they said. As you process, reflect on your child's thoughts and feelings rather than worrying about conveying your own (for example, say, "I hear you saying..." or, "It seems that you may be feeling..."). This will lead to an ongoing conversation, one you can pick up over and over again and add to as you grow to know each other more fully.

HELPFUL PROMPTS

Having a script to follow can make conversations easier. Try any of the following prompts with your child to get started. And if the child's response is weak, give him time.

How are you feeling?

You okay?

Do you want to talk?

Anything going on?

I am feeling _____ [emotional temperature]. How about you?

I had a _____ day. How about you?

I really liked _____ [something good that happened that day]. What happened today that was cool? How did it make you feel?

I had a _____ [something difficult] today and it felt _____. Have you ever had that happen?

When I was younger, I remember feeling _____ when I was _____. (For example: When I was younger, I remember my boyfriend dumped me the day before the junior prom. I cried in the bathroom and felt very sad and worthless. Then, I spoke to some friends, and a friend of mine stepped in to be my date, and I ended up having a great time. So you never really know how things can turn out in the end. There are always surprise endings.)

I am here and I want to help. Can I hold you? Let's take a deep breath together.

Please speak more slowly. I am here for you.

What would you like me to do? How can I help you with this?

Use these follow-up prompts after a conversation to assess:

What went well?

What did not go well?

What was positive/negative?

What could we have done differently?

Did you learn anything?

PART II

· · · · · · · · · · · ·

LET'S TALK:

COMMON
CONCERNS THAT
COME UP
EVERY DAY

In Part 1 we established the need for talking with your kids and gave you general strategies to get you started. Here is where we dig in to the daily conversations. The next five chapters walk you through topics likely to come up in each type of conversation and show you how to approach them. In each chapter, we'll introduce the topic together with several activities that serve as entry points into the subject. We provide prompts to use if you're feeling stuck, as well as an example of a real-world conversation that takes you through the twists and turns these thorny issues can take.

This book can also be used as a reference—simply turn to the spot you need for the topic on your mind. For example, if your child is having difficulty identifying and trusting friends, skip to the discussion and prompts on friendships in Chapter 5. The prompts provide specific questions and lay the groundwork for rich and meaningful conversations.

"THEY MAY FORGET
WHAT YOU SAID–
BUT THEY WILL NEVER
FORGET HOW YOU
MADE THEM FEEL."

CARL W. BUEHNER

Chapter 5

OPENING HEART-BASED CONVERSATIONS

· · · · · · · · · · · · ·

When I was in middle school, my best friend dumped me. I was devastated. I didn't instinctively go to my parents, and in fact felt I couldn't tell anyone because I was so humiliated. She was my whole social life, and when she dumped me I didn't want to go to school. I had no idea how to cope.

That evening my mother and sister, thinking I had already gone to sleep, were heading to bed and found me in my room, sobbing quietly to myself. They asked what was wrong and I told them. I remember their response was definitely concern, but in an "Oh, thank goodness she's not really hurt" kind of way. They knew I would get over this pain, and that knowledge helped me to understand this was not the end of the world. Just sharing my burden helped.

They gave me some ideas: reach out to my friend, ask if she wants to be friends again, and so on. And while those suggestions didn't fix my situation, they helped me plan my next moves, which got me to school and through my classes. I reached out and tried to "get back together" with my best friend, and I recall the pitiful feeling of crawling back. But having that plan helped. And while we didn't become best friends again, I knew I had tried and I had my mother and sister to lean on. They didn't have all the answers—and the answers they did have hadn't accomplished what I wanted. But they offered the empathy and comfort I needed to move forward, and I got to where I needed to be.

EMOTIONS AND THE HEART

Emotions and the heart are linked inextricably. Consider the language we use to describe our emotional states: "My heart hurts," "I am heartbroken," "My heart aches," and "I wish with all my heart..." How we deal with emotional highs and hurts is a determining factor in our level of success and happiness in life. Some people feel incapacitated by very small challenges or disappointments, like forgetting a homework assignment, while others have enormous resiliency and are able to weather huge emotional storms. We want our children to have the strength and resilience to get through everything life throws at them. Helping your child understand her emotional life and develop the necessary skills for navigating the ever-changing waters of adolescence is a keystone of parenting.

Help your child identify and name her feelings. The more you talk together about your emotions, the better support you will be for each other. Model empathy and coping strategies. When my son's girlfriend dumped him he was a little mopey. He didn't tell me what was going on—and, in fact, I learned about the breakup from his ex's mother. I talked with him about it, and instead of telling him I knew how he felt (we can't fully understand someone's else's feelings), I told him that when I'm sad and can't do anything about it I like to watch television and eat ice cream. That may not be the healthiest coping mechanism, but it set us up for a nice evening together and gave us a jumping off point for a conversation about his true feelings.

When our first pet, a guinea pig named Sammy, died, I was really surprised by my son's reaction. He mourned her death in dramatic fashion. After she passed in my arms, my son flung himself on the ground and screamed, "Oh God, please take me instead! She is such a beautiful creature, so full of life. It is not her time!" He went through some of the Kübler-Ross stages of grief, such as anger and denial (further outlined in the sidebar opposite). He bounced among the emotions rapidly throughout the following month, and he still repeats some of the memories of that day if an event triggers him.

My daughter was also very upset but did not have such an extreme reaction. She was more focused on making sure we went out to get another guinea pig as a companion for the one who was "widowed." For both kids, Sammy's was the first death of a being that was very close to them, and they had such different reactions. A child's personality, developmental stage, and emotional reactivity play important parts in his or her emotional reaction to any event. Sometimes events generate strong emotions, and we need to go with the flow and do our best to provide the strong grounding our children need.

DEALING WITH GRIEF

Psychiatrist Elizabeth Kübler-Ross established the five stages of grief, drawing from her work with terminally ill patients. These stages represent the preeminent understanding of how people experience losses of many kinds, including death, divorce, and breakups. In Kübler-Ross's research, she found that people don't necessarily go through the stages in order, but rather they feel all of these emotions at different times of the process. The five stages are listed below:

1. Denial: The person does not accept the loss.

2. Anger: The person experiences rage and strong emotion about the loss.

3. Bargaining. The person offers changes or other sacrifices to make the situation right.

4. Depression: The person becomes despondent and sad over the loss.

5. Acceptance: The person accepts the loss and begins to move on.

FIRST RELATIONSHIPS

Heart-based conversations are crucial in defining and maintaining relationships. The relationship you have with your child is the foundation for all other relationships in his life. According to attachment theory, as postulated by psychologists, John Bowlby and Mary Ainsworth, a child's ability to securely attach to an adult begins within the first year of life. Patterns of consistent love, attention, and caring create this secure bond or attachment.

According to attachment theory, parents who are inconsistent in their care of their child create anxious-resistant bonds. These parents may sometimes be attuned to their child's needs and at other times neglectful of their child's needs. Children raised in this type of environment are typically not trusting of their parents, which can lead them to demonstrate clingy and/or insecure behavior as they look for attention and comfort. Sometimes, children with anxious-resistant bonds avoid seeking contact with their parents and, later, tend to avoid people in general.

Attachment theorists claim that these very early patterns of behavior and bonds carry over to adult romantic relationships and that this relationship pattern becomes a "working model" that each person utilizes in all relationships throughout their lifetime. Therefore, it is essential that we take the time to develop and nurture rock-steady bonds with our children. They will learn how to love, care for, and understand others through their primary relationship with us. This also means they will learn how to argue, disagree, and hurt others based on how they interact with us.

The relationship you have with your spouse, partner, or other close friends and family you co-parent with sets the framework for your child's relationships in the future. And, if you're reading this and panicking because you don't think you've provided a strong model, we can assure you that the very fact you're reading this book suggests you care enough to be good enough. You can break a pattern of dysfunctional relationships—start with your children and rebuild the foundation, but it does take effort and consistency.

Friendships are key for tweens and teens. Your kids' friends and peers are their role models, fan base, and biggest critics. Your child attempts to strike the balance between fitting in and standing out among her peers daily. Her friends are the people she can trust and go to in times of need. Respect that your child depends on her friends, sometimes more than she depends on you. Kids crave approval from peers, even if you want your child to be her own independent person. All that said, your child still needs you, and you are a safe place for her to turn to. While she wants friends' approval, she also needs your love, comfort, and guidance. Remember, you are the parent, not a friend.

A very important aspect of friendship is developing interpersonal skills and conflict management. Friends can be a reflection of your child—get to know your kid's friends, and their families if you can. Rather than worry about the influence other tweens and teens have on your child, try to understand them and enjoy the friendship your child shares with them. You don't have to be the "cool" mom or dad, but make an effort to know the kids in your child's circle. Make time to be with them, and make them comfortable in your home.

You love your child unconditionally. And, even though you sometimes don't like to be with your child, you are there for her when push comes to shove. She cannot simply depend on your love, though—she must also learn to love herself. It's important to help your child develop a relationship with herself. This means she needs to begin to understand who she is and what that means.

Kids need to love themselves and care for themselves. Once they have respect for themselves, they will better understand how their actions represent who they are and how their behavior affects their relationships. And you can help to develop your child's self-love by talking about how you love your child. The greatest gift we can give to someone else is the feeling that they are understood by another human. Your love will offer your child a model for how she can love herself.

INTIMACY

Building intimacy takes time and trust. For your child, it starts with the relationship between the two of you, in the give-and-take of emotions, trust, and empathy. You can't control when your child will be moved to connect with you, so look for those opportunities and be ready to seize them.

Start by being a good model in your intimate relationships. Are you kind and loving to others? Do you care for your own family members and friends? Do you allow your child to express himself freely? This doesn't mean he has to get his way, but that you listen to his perspective and respond in a respectful way. Do you admit when you're wrong and help your child to see when he is wrong? Avoid holding your child's errors over his head for a long period—this will help him to see that he can make mistakes, learn from them, and move on, and that you're someone he can go to through thick and thin.

Share your own feelings and welcome his—even the angry ones. Try to help your child understand and label his own feelings without naming them yourself. And finally, help him by working through problems with him, being a cheer-leader, and showing him that you believe in him.

Intimacy can include both friendships and romantic relationships. Intimacy looks different at different ages and with different people, and as your child ages, he will experience deeper, more intimate relationships with a broader set of people. It's tempting to slow him down. You might not want your son to date, for example, because you're concerned that he will lose focus on school and friendships. You may not want your daughter to have one best friend because you're afraid she won't socialize with a group and if something goes wrong she will be without a friend. While it's good to teach your children to exercise cau-tion when it comes to intimate relationships, you don't want to discourage them from forging deep bonds with others. Rather than discourage relationships, question your child about them. And teach your kids to question themselves. "Do you trust this person?" "Why?" "What gives you pause?"

Often, we link intimacy and sex. And, while sex can be a truly intimate act, it is not the only way our children will find intimacy with others. Some parents pre-fer their children not develop close relationships outside the family or postpone dating until a certain age. Recognize that each child is different, and some can handle situations that others of the same age cannot. So, rather than teaching your child to avoid intimacy or trying to delay it, talk with your child about how to be intimate with others.

Dating can mean many things, and it offers an opportunity for your child to test different relationships and form his own identity. You know your child best, and if he doesn't seem ready to you, then talk about it. Explain why you'd like him to hold off instead of setting a simple "no dating" rule. Perhaps you can come up with a solution that works for everyone. For example, if he is determined to date a specific person, get to know him or her and set limits for what constitutes a date. Maybe he could invite friends along.

Dating is not synonymous with sex, and you should make that clear to your son or daughter. It's okay to set expectations, but let your child be a part of establishing those as well. You can't control your child's physical urges or romantic inclinations, so help him to understand that those desires will play into his decisions and that he has choices. It might help him to know what you hope for him, and to have some of his own expectations; for example, you might tell him you want him to be able to trust the person he is intimate with.

CONNECTING IN THE DIGITAL AGE

Real, deep human connection for tweens and teens is becoming a rarity. These are the days of quick texts, emojis, Snapchat, and visual posts as a way of connecting with others. Many teens and adults are even intimidated by making phone calls or leaving a voicemail. A text or email is much more controllable and predictable. People consciously and subconsciously choose quick and easy social connections (much like a fast food meal), rather than deep, long, slow social connections (like a delicious, healthy, home-cooked meal). Instinctively, we know that the result of this choice is a bloated, empty, and unfulfilling life—but, because the phenomenon is relatively new, we have yet to understand the full effect of an unwholesome social media diet.

When it comes to building relationships of the heart, technology can sometimes be helpful, but at other times it can act as a distraction from, or a barrier to, a conversation. The best way to help your child understand the pros and cons is to embrace technology and embark on the journey with him. Communicate in person but also via your child's preferred technology so you have a sense of how your child communicates with his peers. This also sets you up for a great conversation about when it's helpful and when it's hurtful or counterproductive to communicate digitally.

I've had the opportunity to connect with my kids in ways I never could have before technology. I can do quick check-ins and they can vent to me when they need to. Texts or digital chats can also provide a platform for funny banter where we can enjoy each other. The important thing is to follow up on big topics and not rely on technology as the chief means of communication with your child.

OPENING OURSELVES UP

Connection and intimacy cannot grow unless an open heart and vulnerability are present. In the book *Daring Greatly*, researcher Brené Brown suggests vulnerability is not weakness, and the uncertainty, risk, and emotional exposure we face every day are not optional. Opening up to another person makes you vulnerable, and taking the steps to trust someone with your innermost thoughts and feelings requires exceptional bravery. When we expose ourselves in this way, we take a risk that we will be hurt or damaged. But we also understand that this level of deep connection is the lifeblood of our emotional center. You can't simply manufacture trust. It is the foundation of heart-based connection and needs to be fostered through these conversations.

Deep connection only happens when we take a chance and share something emotionally risky with another person. This is the process of relationship building. One person puts the feelers out and tests the waters with another person, hoping that the other's reaction is open, comforting, and validating. The strongest relationships ebb and flow, with one person unfolding and trusting and the other person listening and receiving, and then the roles switch. We typically will start with smaller morsels and then graduate to problems or feelings we are really struggling with. Bonding happens when the relationship reaches a new level of trust and connection, and the two people feel very aligned, with few barriers between them. This is when the relationship has a natural flow.

Much of the research and thinking on heart-based relationships has roots in marriage and family therapy. The principles for building a healthy relationship are the same, whether the relationship is with a romantic partner, child, or friend. The boundaries—and the roles you and the other person play—in each of these relationships are, of course, drastically different. This is something to keep in mind moving forward. For example, when talking with your child about what makes a relationship a healthy one, you might note that any healthy relationship has a high level of trust, shared values, and connection. But the boundaries and levels of intimacy will change depending on the type of relationship and the interest in the connection.

Talking with your children about boundaries and when to trust certain people with private information is very important. Some teens might need to know it's okay not to tell everyone everything about themselves (too-loose boundaries)

Inspiration

During heart-based conversations:

Support friendships whether or not you like your child's friends.

Be a parent, not a friend.

Encourage and model self-love.

Name emotions you're feeling and encourage your child to talk about hers.

Celebrate self-awareness.

Lean in to intimacy.

Use metaphors and stories in conversations.

ASSESSMENT: WHICH EMOTIONAL TYPE IS YOUR CHILD?

Use this assessment as a way of better understanding how your child generally reacts to strong emotions. People are typically not categorized as just one type, so it is normal for your child to generally be a stuffer, but, given the right circumstances, to be an exploder. These types are not absolutes, but rather provide a guide to help you develop greater understanding and self-awareness.

Question: It is the weekend and you planned on taking your children sledding, but it is raining and you have to cancel your plans. What is the typical reaction your child will have?

Exploder reaction: "Erupt in the moment." He becomes very upset and does not understand how or why the change in plans happened. In an hour or two, the child may let go of the negativity. In this case, it is good to remember that all storms pass and offer your child a distraction in the meantime.

Brewer reaction: "It's fine, but..." This child may automatically say the change is fine but then later on in the day, she may ask again why the original plans changed. She may also ask when she will be able to go sledding again and may perseverate until she has an answer. This child may worry about the change in plans and how it will affect the rest of the weekend.

Stuffer reaction: "That's okay." This child will simply move on with the rest of the day. Later, the child may feel uncomfortable, but is not likely to recognize why. This child needs help identifying and being comfortable with her feelings.

Question: Your child comes home from school and says that he made a mistake on a test at school. What is the typical reaction your child will have?

Erupter reaction: Anger outburst. This child may yell and scream and even put the blame on other people, like the teacher or you. Allow the emotion to unfold and check in when the child is calmer.

Brewer reaction: Worry wart. This child will discuss the play-by-play of the mistake and its impact. He will take this incident very seriously and need to be soothed to understand that everyone makes mistakes, even adults.

Stuffer reaction: Moving on. This child will brush off the mistake and believe in "better luck next time." The parent of this type of child needs to make space to talk about feelings such as disappointment, but also honor and nourish the child's optimism.

and other teens may need coaxing to open up about themselves (too-tight boundaries). When it comes to intimacy, parents should share their values and thoughts about what an intimate relationship should look like. Children look to their parents for information, structure, and understanding about social relationships, and things that you think may be obvious should be stated and discussed because healthy social connections are essential for your child's happiness and well-being.

The Heart-Based Project
ACTIVITY 1: ASSESS YOUR CHILD'S EMOTIONAL TYPE

How does your child deal with her emotions? Is your child an exploder, a brewer, or a stuffer? You need to know this, but your child also needs to know this about herself. Knowing your tendencies in reacting to situations helps you understand what you say and do. And understanding where your child comes from can help you engage more meaningfully. Do the emotional type assessment with your child and decide which type she is—and think about what type you are. Talk about how your type might affect how you engage with each other and others in joyful, sad, and stressful situations.

Exploder. Exploders are enthusiastic and extroverted. Their moods can shift quickly and be infectious. They will share lots of excitement and can also erupt quickly when difficult emotions come up. These children may also recover from upsets quickly. Exploders are more likely to be male. These children need to learn appropriate expression and should celebrate their enthusiasm. Exploders need space and time to defuse their emotions and process events when they are ready.

Brewer. Brewers are thoughtful and careful. They can process a lot of thoughts before sharing, and this can create anxiety. They often roll with the flow but, when they worry, they stew and have trouble managing the worry. These children need to process changes and should celebrate their thoughtful approach. Brewers need to learn how to let things—and thoughts—go. They tend to be anxious children and benefit from taking stock in their previous resilience in action, learning to "unhook" from emotional states, and learning to let go of spinning thoughts.

Stuffer. Stuffers are kind to others and allow them to shine. They like to hide their feelings and feed off of others' feelings. They often put difficult or emotional thoughts in a hypothetical box and put the box high up in the closet. Stuffers like to be busy so they don't have to pay attention to anything uncomfortable. They tend to present as if they are totally in control. These children are more likely to be female. They will need more work in developing mutual emotional language and should celebrate their calm manner, which likely helps others around them.

ACTIVITY 2: DIG DEEP INTO RELATIONSHIPS

Find a moment with your child when it's just the two of you (shopping, in the car, or maybe just push pause on the television) and you have a few minutes to dig deep. Take this opportunity to check in with your child about her friendships. Try starting with, "Who do you truly trust?" See where the conversation goes and make an effort to really listen.

If your child is romantically involved, take this moment to check her emotional temperature. You are looking to see if she feels safe in the relationship and if she is happy, but straightforward questions don't always get to the heart of the matter. Try starting with, "What is one thing you really enjoy about being in your relationship?" As the conversation continues, check in with, "Is there anything you think I should know about you and [fill in the name of the significant other]?" Before you end the conversation, make sure your child knows she has someone she can go to, if not you, should she have questions about the relationship. And if you think she already knows, remind her with something like, "Don't forget, if you have any questions and you don't want to talk with me about it, you can always call [insert the name of your go-to person]."

ACTIVITY 3: NAME THAT EMOTION

Sometimes it is difficult to label feelings and emotions, but conversations are easier if we have an emotional language to use. Take some time to talk with your child about emotions and how to identify them. Here's a way to get started: "Let's list some feelings you might have had today and I will work on my own list. Then we will get together and compare our lists to see if we use the same names for feelings." Note that you might need to describe emotions in detail to see if you're describing the same ones.

Another idea is to print out a list of emojis and, with your child, name the feeling/emotion associated with each emoji—make sure you have an expanded list. Have fun with this list. For example, happy might be "get jiggy with it," feeling brave might be "roaring like a lion," feeling silly might be "laughing like a monkey," and so on.

We want to work on expanding the rainbow of feelings and emotions, so aim to use lots of words and talk about the many different emotional shades of each.

In Practice: USING METAPHORS IN CONVERSATION

Metaphors allow people to eloquently visualize the emotions, feelings, and growth that are the internal work of therapy. I like to use metaphors found in nature because they are rich and illustrative. Try peppering them into conversations to help your child understand her internal, psychological, emotional world. Below are some popular ones I use in therapy:

Rainbow of feelings. Have your kid think of a rainbow and identify the feelings that would be associated with the different colors. For example, what would a blue kind of day mean to you? Remember, kids may have their own interpretation of colors. For example, blue might mean sad to one kid and elated to another. Later, when you establish what the different colors mean to your child, you can use them as a code to ask how her day was. For example, "What color was your day and why?"

Storms. Storms are another great metaphor. Watch a thunderstorm together and talk about how explosive weather can be a lot like explosive emotions—with lightning (rage), torrential downpours (tears), and damaging wind (pain and disappointment). The best part is that a storm does not last forever and there is often a beautiful sunset in the end. This is a great metaphor for the lesson that resilience, strength, and happiness are products of pain, struggle, and obstacles overcome.

Surfing. I love surfing as a metaphor for understanding the unpredictability and changeability of life. Have your child imagine a day at the beach, with big waves coming in from the ocean. As a surfer, you don't know what wave comes and when, but you prepare the best you can and try to stay on top of the wave. Inevitably, you will fall off the board at times, but it is your job to keep getting up. It is all part of becoming a surfer of waves and a surfer of life.

CONVERSATION STARTERS AND PROMPTS

Here are some prompts and talking points for starting a heart-based conversation with your child:

EMOTIONS

Reminisce about a time when you hurt your child or maybe your child hurt you, and talk about how you both felt. What helped resolve the feeling? Is it resolved? Sometimes digging back to the early years can make this a fun conversation.

"Tell me about a time you felt hurt. What happened? How did you feel? For how long?"

"What thoughts/actions/behaviors helped move you through this? How did you get better? What did not help?"

FAMILY

Ask your child what she thinks about your family or how she fits in. Talk about when you were young, and share stories of your relationships with your siblings, cousins, aunts, uncles, and others. Share why you started your family. What was the situation? Why did you want kids? How did you feel when your child was born?

"Do we have any family traditions you love?"

"Is there anything we do as a family that you'd want to continue with your own family when you're older?"

"Have I ever told you about the time that I _____?"

"Did you know that your grandfather was a _____?"

FRIENDSHIPS

Nurture your child's friendships and be open if you don't think they are always good friendships. Acknowledge feelings—"I know this hurts"—and assure your child that it's okay to be disappointed or angry with a friend. Make sure kids understand that being angry doesn't mean the friendship is over: "We don't always say or act the way we should—focus on the solution."

"What makes a good friend?"

"Who do you feel you can really depend on?"

"Do you see yourself being friends as adults?"

"Are you still hanging out with _____? What is she up to?/Why not?"

"How do you know if a person is bad/toxic/unhealthy? Are there signs in your body/mind? What does your gut say?"

"Do you ever feel like someone is trying to convince you to do things you are not proud of, or that you don't want to do?"

"Tell me about a time you chose to stop being friends with someone. How do you part with a friend?"

Be patient and calm when talking about intimacy. Avoid judgment and too much advice right off the bat. Remember, family relationships and friendships can be intimate as well.

"When you think about a relationship with a boy or girl in the future what do you picture? How do you feel? What things do you enjoy doing together? What qualities does this person have?"

"What relationships have you seen or experienced that were healthy? What did they look like? What elements did they have?"

"How do kids tell other kids they like them?"

"How do you know you are in love?"

"What relationships have you seen or experienced that were unhealthy? What did they look like? How did you know they were unhealthy?"

"How do you know when to stay in a relationship and when you need to get out? How can you break it off?" (Share a story about a hard breakup.)

"What is dating? What does it mean to you?"

"Is monogamy important?"

"What ways can you show love to another person? To yourself?"

"What are the ways you show me that you love me?"

"What are the ways I show you that I love you?"

LOSS AND GRIEF

Loss is something we don't talk about a lot, yet it affects everyone. People grieve in different ways, and you should be prepared to talk with your child about loss even if you prefer to grieve alone. The subject may arise when you are not expecting it, so it's good to lay the groundwork for your child to come to you.

"Do you ever think about [name someone who has passed away]? What do you miss most about them?"

Share a story about a time when you lost someone and how you feel about this loss.

SELF-LOVE

Self-love is not conceit. In fact, it's essential for building a good relationship with yourself and others.

"Do you love yourself? Why?"

"Why do you think we sometimes value qualities like bravery, honesty, taking risks, and vulnerability in other people but not in ourselves?"

"Would you say that to a friend or to me? Do you think it is okay to be harsh, critical, or mean to yourself?" (Say this in response to a child being harshly self-critical.)

TRUST

Remember that trust takes time to build. These conversations will help you build trust with your child, and you should also talk about how she can build trust with others. Ask questions about who your child trusts and why—and ask follow-up questions.

"Who do you trust?"

"Who don't you trust?"

"How do you know you can trust someone?"

"Do you trust everyone who is close to you?"

"What are some ways you can figure out if you can trust another person?"

CONVERSATION IN ACTION

Your thirteen-year-old daughter comes home from school and bursts into tears as soon as you ask her how her day was. You instinctively ask, "What's wrong?" She starts to mention her friend and then answers, "Nothing," and shuts herself in her room. You knock on the door and press her for information, and she yells at you to back off. She adds that her life is over now. "I don't have any friends, since my best friend has basically excommunicated me!" What now?

First things first. If she is in her room and asked you to stay out, give her space. Time will help her feel better, even if it won't resolve the issue. Resist the urge to call her friend or her friend's parents to get more info on the situation. This will signal to your child that you don't have her back, and sometimes more information is not helpful. After giving her some time and space, identify a good time to chat. Try to re-engage her when she seems more settled. If bedtime rolls around and you still haven't seen her, insist on at least saying goodnight. Here are a few good ways to get the conversation going and to keep it going:

Acknowledge her pain and avoid trying to solve her problem for her.

"I can see you're hurting. Do you want to just sit together? Can I get you anything?"

"Friendships are relationships, and they take turns that can sometimes be hard to navigate."

"You can only control you—what would help you right now?"

Show concern and ask what happened, but accept that you may not get all the details. You don't need the details to help her.

"What happened?"

"Do you feel like talking about it?"

"Is there something you want to share?"

"Is there someone you would prefer to talk to?"

"Do you want to write down your thoughts?"

Understand that friendships vary and relationships change, as much for your child as they do for you. Support her in dealing with confrontation and problem-solving, and help her accept that not all friendships survive conflict.

"Do you have a sense of your friend's perspective?"

"What do you think your friend would say about what happened?"

"Do you feel comfortable talking to your friend? Would it be easier to call or text?"

Give your child time to respond. And, if she prefers not to share, that's okay for the time being. Let her know you are there for her and she has options if she doesn't want to share with you.

"I love you no matter what happens between you and your friends."

"When you're ready to talk, I will be here for you."

"It's good to share when you're ready. Even if you choose not to talk to me, I hope you will share with someone."

Offer a distraction, not to make everything all better, but to show her life will go on. The distraction could be as simple as joining her for a walk, or it could be something more elaborate, like taking her for a meal, a movie, or another outing she'd enjoy.

"We'd love you to join us for dinner and at least just sit with us, even if you're not hungry."

"Let's go out for a little treat—where would you like to go? What do you want to do?"

Throughout the next days, weeks, and months, keep to a "normal" schedule and try not to focus too heavily on the concern of the friendship unless she brings it up. Return to the conversation occasionally, showing your daughter that you recognize this is a big deal and that she has somewhere to go to talk about it. But it also takes the main spotlight off the trauma in her life and helps her to move on.

"COMFORT ZONES ARE MOST OFTEN EXPANDED THROUGH DISCOMFORT."

PETER MCWILLIAMS

Chapter 6

NAVIGATING UNCOMFORTABLE CONVERSATIONS

When I told my friend, Mary, that I was writing a book about conversations with kids she brightened up and said, "Have I got a story for you!" Mary talked about her sassy middle daughter, Emme, who peaked early in her development in many ways. When Emme was in fourth grade, Mary was called into the principal's office totally out of the blue.

Emme had never been in trouble before, so my friend had no idea what could have happened. The principal asked her to come to school to pick up a book that Emme and a friend had been working on during their bus rides. Apparently, the girls were turned in by a third classmate who felt excluded from the project. Mary asked the principal to please just send the book home, but the principal refused. When she entered the principal's office, everyone was very serious and concerned. The staff went on to explain that her sweet fourth grader was working on a book about sex that included explicit stories and *illustrations*. Mary didn't know her daughter could draw so well.

While the school staff seemed flabbergasted, Mary found herself laughing, "Well, maybe she will get a job at *Playboy* someday." The school staff did not seem amused, but Emme's mom saw no benefit from quashing her daughter's spirit and creativity. The book opened up a conversation about sex and sexuality, as well as appropriate ways to express oneself on many different levels. Mary kept the book and is thrilled that she had the opportunity to start a conversation she didn't realize her daughter was ready to have. This example reinforces why we should start talking about sex with our children early, and continue often—because the information is already at their fingertips.

IDENTIFYING YOUR COMFORT ZONE—AND LEAVING IT

Just as our kids do not want to think about their parents having sex, we do not want to think about our kids as sexual beings. Merely acknowledging your discomfort in talking about sex or other potentially awkward topics can be very helpful—it's good for your child to understand that you're not comfortable, and, yet, you are having this conversation. Your child needs to know that he can come to you with questions—and if he feels he can't go to you, he should identify a person he can talk to (see Chapter 3 for more about identifying a go-to person). Continuing with the conversation, even though it brings you out of your comfort zone, shows your child that he can't just ignore uncomfortable situations himself.

We ask our children to leave their comfort zones multiple times a day. For some, it's walking through the cafeteria looking for a safe place to sit. For others, it's speech class where they are forced to practice public speaking or answer off-the-cuff questions. They change location, situation, and context as often as every forty-five minutes, depending on school schedules. And we ask them to be on task, prepared, and motivated for whatever is to come. They balance their social lives, academics, and extracurricular activities, along with family obligations, sleep, and, hopefully, some down time. If we expect them to leave their comfort zones so regularly, we should be ready to leave ours as well—and that often involves talking with them about challenging matters.

We all love to be comfortable, cozy, and stable. As humans, we avoid discomfort and pain; these things are destabilizing, and we look for ways we can take away the pain when we are hurt. Sometimes this hurt can cause anxiety, depression, and even trauma. Our motivation for seeking comfort and avoiding discomfort has a long history in psychology. But as a psychologist, I also know that growth, resilience, and strength are born out of the sticky, icky place of discomfort, and that true happiness resides on the other side of struggle. As my

BECOME COMFORTABLE WITH DISCOMFORT

Think about growth for a moment. For plants, animals, and humans, growing pains are very real. Growth hurts and feels awkward. This same template for physical growth can be applied to mental and emotional growth. In my clinical work, I recommend that clients "flex their mental muscles" and challenge themselves to do tasks that are outside their comfort zones. Some examples might include asking a friend to join them for coffee, telling themselves a positive affirmation every morning, practicing deep-breath meditation, or visualizing themselves succeeding at their goals.

People can get caught in patterns and ways of operating in the world that are not conducive to positive growth, and new healthy habits can feel different. I remind my clients that it takes six weeks to break a habit, and consistency is key. Feeling uncomfortable just means you are growing.

yoga teacher would say, "The most blessed blossom, the lotus, can only grow in dark, muddy waters."

There's really no trick to jumping into an uncomfortable conversation—you need to just decide to do it. And if a hard-to-have conversation gets to be too much, consider taking a break. Just make sure you return to the talk you need to have.

MANAGING MEDIA

A big benefit brought on by the digital age is that we have access to lots of information on every topic—but that load of information can also be a problem. It's our job as parents to teach our children how to manage media and think critically about the information they consume. This includes managing media timewise, but also considering quality—what makes something worth your time or a waste of time? What can you trust as true and what might be questionable? Talk about what your child processes online as much as you talk about what she processes offline.

When you're having uncomfortable conversations, use examples from media to help you illustrate points you want to make that might be hard to find in real life or might require you to share too much experience. Bring up examples of behavior in movies, the news, and television shows that help stress your viewpoint. It can be a relief to point to someone else's bad choices or unfortunate circumstances rather than constantly relying on examples from your own past or pointing out how your child is disappointing you. Ask your child for his opinions on these current events—kids often will surprise you with a perspective you hadn't thought of.

While we want our children to understand how to have conversations and hold eye contact, we can also use our dependence on our devices to our advantage for some uncomfortable conversations. Know that you have to connect in reality at some point, but it's okay to send digital reminders or check-ins to your child that might be easier done without eye contact, or that you simply might not have the opportunity to say when you need to most. For example, if your daughter is at a party, send an encouraging text reminding her to refrain from drinking and sex; or, if you think she will make those choices, send a text with reminders about how to stay safe (never drive if you've been drinking; use birth control).

One concerning area of media for teens and tweens is pornography. Your child will likely be exposed to sexually explicit content at some point, either by accident or on purpose. Recognize that, depending on the sources, your child may view unrealistic and disturbing images of sex, which can create a dysfunctional foundation for sexual development.

Recent research suggests that consumption of pornography is associated with many negative emotional, psychological, and physical health outcomes. These may include increased rates of depression and anxiety, acting out, violent behavior, sexual behavior at an early age, sexual promiscuity, a higher risk of teen pregnancy, and a dysfunctional view of relationships. Sex is a strong drive to connect deeply with other humans, and if your child watches pornography regularly, he may learn inappropriate and unhealthy ways of connecting. Try redirecting him to other, more social activities but also be willing to reach out for professional help.

APPROACHING TRANSITIONS

As humans, we are creatures of habit. Life is easier and more comfortable when we know what to expect. Changes in our routine can throw us off our game and make it hard for us to be as people expect us to be. During times of transition—changing schools, moving homes, enduring illness or grief, or going through separation and divorce—we have to overcome our own discomfort and help our children ease into the change. Be up front and honest with your child, and acknowledge the change head on. Come up with strategies to make the transition as comfortable as possible. For example, if you're moving or your child has to change schools abruptly, find out as much as you can about the new school, and visit with your child. Join groups in the new neighborhood, even if your actions feel forced, so that when you arrive you will have something to do with your children.

In times of transition, our emotions can take hold and we may doubt ourselves. In response to the uncertainty around them, kids can feel frustrated and confused, which can make them appear withdrawn, moody, sad, angry, or defiant. When major life changes are happening, parents need to remain as stable and steady as possible as the kids work through their emotional storms. Sometimes, because so much is changing, just acknowledging the turmoil and being there is all a parent can do. During this time, it is also important for parents to receive support and guidance for themselves.

ANSWER HONESTLY AND OPENLY

When kids have questions, answer everything you can—within reason. It's okay to push the conversation to a better time if you are feeling harried, but don't ignore a topic just because it makes you feel funny.

TITILLATING DINNER CONVERSATION

We were out to dinner with a family friend and were talking about high school parties and the possibility of sex. My fourteen-year-old daughter chimed in, "Can women have erections?" I was completely caught off guard. I didn't think so. Maybe. Is a stimulated clitoris considered an erection? Is there a name for it?

I realized that, though versed in child development, I was totally unprepared for the question. I blushed and made an effort to answer her with what I knew about sexual stimulation of the female body. The time and place were not the most appropriate, and having my ten-year-old son and family friend present did not help matters. However, my daughter's question may never have come out had it been just us. So I answered to the best of my ability and noted to myself that I needed to look up some more terminology.

I found a time and place to talk with my daughter at length about how the female body responds during sex. The setting was private and the conversation more awkward because we were not having a casual interaction like we had been in at the restaurant. But I was able to say the rest of what I wished I had said in the restaurant, and she knew the conversation was important enough to me to get back to it.

When we were going for an ultrasound, my then three-year-old daughter asked, "How did the baby get in there?" I prided myself on being the mom who shared anything and everything, and I was so happy to have the conversation. But lying on a hospital bed, with a technician and my parents in the room, was not ideal for this conversation. So at first I laughed awkwardly and looked everywhere I could without looking anywhere. My daughter would not relent—good for her! I told her that it was a great question, and I would answer it when we got home. When we did have the conversation, I wanted her to know it was me and not her that made it weird, so I told her that while we could definitely talk about it, I was more comfortable having that conversation in private.

No matter how awkward you may feel, let your child know that your discomfort is not because of her, and that even though you do feel weird, it's okay to have the conversation. This shows your child that she can come to you even when she is concerned you may be uncomfortable or she may feel ill at ease.

So when the Viagra commercials come on or you hear reference in the news to inappropriate behavior from a celebrity, don't hope it goes over your child's head. Stop and talk. React. Laugh if you need to. Cry if you need to. And have the conversation. Make sure you show your child that this warrants your time and energy.

Inspiration

During uncomfortable conversations:

Acknowledge discomfort.

Step outside your comfort zone.

Be honest and direct.

Notice transitions and their effects.

Understand and respect consent.

Admit when you don't know something. You don't know everything, so why pretend? Find the answers, and teach your child to look for them—perhaps you can find some of them together. This search for answers will help your child see how you filter and vet information and how you determine what sources are reliable. If you realize later that you didn't say all you had to say on the matter, there is no harm in going back to the conversation and clarifying.

The Uncomfortable Project

ACTIVITY 1: MOVIE NIGHT

Find a time to watch a show or movie with your teen. Make an effort to find something out of your comfort zone; it could be in a genre not usually to your taste, it could have adult themes, or it could be more violent than you're used to. Make sure the choice is, for whatever reason, something you wouldn't ordinarily watch—or at least that you wouldn't view with your teen. If you're feeling extra brave, have your child help you pick one. Stop and talk about what's going on throughout the show or movie. Pause the action to talk about the choices the characters make. If there is a sex scene, note that it looks one way on the screen, but that should not set an expectation for reality.

ACTIVITY 2: HAVING THE TALK

You are your child's first educator, and that makes you his first sex educator as well. If you haven't already, start that conversation about the birds and the bees. Research suggests that sex education is associated with a delay in having sex, as well as with healthier sexual behaviors when teens do start. So, while you may be uncomfortable, jump in and get going. If you don't help kids understand this topic, they will get their information from another source—and that information may be scary, misleading, or wildly inaccurate. The more kids know, the better they can take care of themselves.

Start talking with your kid about bodies and relationships in an age-appropriate way when they are young, so that the conversation is as natural as possible as they grow older and the topic becomes more urgent. Revisit the conversation often so you both have lots of practice asking and answering questions.

Offer up the basics of body changes, sex, and sexual acts, so your child understands what you are talking about. Don't be coy and talk around the subject. This is your opportunity to educate and share your personal values. Help your child understand that you have certain values in your home and that he will eventually develop his own, which may be different. Assure your child that just because he is having sex does not mean he should feel compelled to continue having sex, either in his current relationship or in another. It's okay to stop having sex, even if you've already started. Don't be afraid to be blunt, and encourage your child to get comfortable with frank language.

Some points you might consider covering in your conversation:

➤ Sex can be a healthy and fun expression of intimacy when both people are mature, emotionally ready, and able to talk with their partner honestly about their decision to have sex and how to protect themselves.

In Practice: HOW OLD IS OLD ENOUGH FOR SEX?

The average age at which kids start having sex is seventeen. And while you might like to assume your child will wait till she is "old enough" (whatever that means to you), you should realize that the average age means that kids are having sex at younger ages as well. The longer kids wait, the more mature they will be and the better they will handle the emotions that come with a sexual relationship. That said, it's important to let teens know that if they do decide to have sex at a young age, they are not doomed to an unhappy life. Early experiences can act as models and comparisons for future relationships, so there is an opportunity for learning from them. Your child is still your child, and you still love her.

➤ Kids can get confused about sex when they aren't sure of the details. Go through the nuts and bolts. Be very clear about what sex is and how it works. You cannot leave this to the movies or your child's peers. Share your own values and your hopes for your child.

➤ Consent is paramount in sexual relationships. Talk about what it looks and sounds like and how to broach the subject, even when your child is uncomfortable. Yes means yes, and if your partner does not give an enthusiastic yes, then you do not have consent.

➤ Safety comes first. Talk to your child about measures they can take to protect themselves from sexually transmitted diseases (STDs) and pregnancy. Whether your preferred method is birth control or abstinence, be prepared to help your child understand and practice responsible behavior.

➤ Relationships are okay. It's important for your child to understand that it's okay to expect and want a relationship with the person you are sleeping with. Kids often feel pressured to have sex, and sometimes begin a sexual connection before there is an emotional one. This pressure can come from their romantic interest, but also from their peers, who may or may not be having sex themselves, as well as from the media.

➤ Oral sex is not a safe alternative to intercourse. While it won't result in pregnancy, it has its own dangers and involves intimacy.

➤ Masturbation is a natural and safe way to explore your body and to get to know yourself better.

ACTIVITY 3: PLAY "I NEVER"

Remember that old drinking game, I Never? Try a fun version with your kid. Start by sharing something you don't think your child would know about you: I've never _____. If your kid has experienced it, then he can take a piece of candy, a penny, or some other small incentive (not a shot!). The catch is, he has to share his experience with you. You don't have to reveal everything, but keep in mind that the more you share, the more likely to open up your child will be. Kids love to hear about back when you were human, too.

Here are some good "I never" statements to start with—feel free to come up with your own:

I've never failed a test before.

I've never asked anyone out on a date.

I've never had a crush on anyone before.

I've never done something I'm ashamed of.

I've never driven too fast in a car.

I've never lied to a teacher/friend/parent.

CONVERSATION STARTERS AND PROMPTS

Here are some prompts and talking points for starting an uncomfortable conversation with your child:

DIVERSITY

It's important to celebrate diversity so your child understands that she can be who she is and learns to respect others and appreciate them for who they are.

"What does diversity mean to you?"

"Do you think that you can understand diversity if you are not a member of a minority?"

"Have you heard racist remarks or seen examples of discrimination? What did you do? Do you wish you did something differently?"

"What does it mean to 'celebrate diversity'? What does this look like?"

"What do you like about yourself?"

"What makes you unique?"

"If you could choose three adjectives to describe yourself, what would
they be?" (Then share three adjectives you would use to describe
your child.)

"What three adjectives would you use to describe me?" (Share three you
might use to describe yourself.)

"What are things that make people weird that are good?"

"If someone annoys you, how can you tell if it's their personality or their
actions—or are they inseparable?"

"Have you ever not liked someone and then grown to know them and
changed your mind? What made you see the person differently?"

DIVORCE/SEPARATION

Ideally, before jumping into a conversation about divorce or separation
with your kids, you will have time to talk with your spouse and set some
expectations. Be clear, direct, and open to questions.

"Dad and I are getting a divorce/separation." (Offer a clear reason, some
ideas of what to expect, and the plans you have so far.)

If the kids are young, explain in concrete terms what divorce/separation
is. Provide a reason for the divorce/separation. This helps kids make sense
of the divorce/separation.

"Do you have any questions?"

FEAR

Share what scares you and inquire what scares your child.

"Has fear ever stopped you from trying something?" If so, ask: "Do you regret that?"

"What do you think it means to live with hope versus to live with fear?"

GENDER AND GENDER IDENTITY

Talk with your child about what it means to be masculine or feminine. If you say someone is "too girly," what does that mean? If you say someone is "manly," what does this mean? Which one is more powerful? How do you define yourself on this scale? Research suggests that a person who demonstrates both feminine and masculine traits is the most well-adjusted type of person. Explore how some people identify clearly with a gender that is consistent with their biological sex, some identify with a gender other than the one assigned to them at birth, and some don't identify with a fixed gender (gender fluid).

"What do you think it means to be gender fluid?"

"Do you know any kids who are gender fluid?"

"Do you ever feel like you're not who other people think you are?"

"Can you imagine feeling like you should be in a different body?"

In addition to the mechanics of sex, talk about what it means to have sex and to be in a sexual relationship. Acknowledge sexuality as a natural part of being human and be sure to answer questions directly.

"Have you thought about having sex?"

"Are any of your friends having sex?"

"Are you having sex? Is that what you want? Do you think it's what your girl/boyfriend wants?"

If your child answers that he is having sex, continue: "Let's talk about (or let's review) what it means to have safe sex. Safe sex means doing your best to keep yourself safe both emotionally and physically." Discuss specific birth control and prevention of sexually transmitted diseases.

"Can you tell me if you're having safe sex and what that means to you?"

"Please come to me if you feel scared or something happens that you need support with (for example, pregnancy, your partner is not on the same page as you, contraction of an STD, or emotional drama)."

"How do you know if someone wants to have sex?"

"You don't need to have sex, even if you've already had it. It's okay to say no, even if you've said yes in the past to the same person or to someone else."

"What does consent look like?" Reiterate that only yes means yes. Remind your child: Unless your partner is enthusiastically saying yes, you do not have consent.

CONVERSATION IN ACTION

You and your spouse are separating and plan to divorce, and your sixteen-year-old son blames Dad because he moved out first, while your thirteen-year-old daughter doesn't know what to make of the situation and reacts with a lot of emotion.

Sit down with your co-parent and your children to acknowledge that you are going through this transition as a family, no matter what the family looks like. Be clear with the facts: You are divorcing, and this is a decision made by the adults about the adult relationship. It is not a reflection on your relationship with your children.

Nothing about this transition will be easy, and interactions might get volatile—your children are processing new information, and it's something you've likely had more time to think through. Your kids might be very angry, sad, or despondent. Think about what your kids have seen or heard and how the situation might appear to them. Have you and your spouse been warm and loving to each other? Have you been distant or arguing with each other? Have interactions with the kids been different for a while? What do your kids know and what might they have picked up on? Be as honest as you can and share, within reason, information that will help them to paint a full picture. For example, if you've tried counseling and gone back and forth on your decision, share that part of the process so your children understand that you are doing your best and seeking support.

> "This is hard for everyone, but we tried to work it out and have not been able to. We have decided to divorce because [insert reasons for divorce if appropriate]."

Share a plan or an outline for next steps, to help prepare your kids. The transition will feel less scary if you all have clear action items. Be sure to include plans for living arrangements in this discussion.

> "This means that you will stay in the house, and Dad and I will alternate who stays here with you. We are looking at alternative homes now and figuring out what we can afford."

Assure your children that they are your number-one concern and you will do what you can to take care of everyone involved. No matter what happens, this is still your family.

> "There will be a lot of emotion. You might be angry. I'm angry (or have been). We need to learn how to manage our feelings and share them. While you are probably angry with us, you need to understand we love you and you can come to us with anything. Let's think of other people you can go to if you want to talk to someone else."

Allow time for the kids to ask any questions and check in about their fears. Typically, the biggest fear for kids is abandonment. Reiterate that you will always be their parent and they are your family forever. Talk about what things will be the same for them, like school, family home, pets, friends, and extended family. The less change there is in the things the kids care about, the easier the transition becomes.

Reaffirm the schedule for the kids.

> "We have worked out a schedule, and you will be with me on Monday and Tuesday and you will be with Mom on Wednesday and Thursday. Every other weekend, you will be with me and the other weekends, you'll be with Mom."

Also, talk about after-school time and activities. Kids' routines and activities are very important to them and give them a sense of stability during this time. Make an effort to keep routines similar to the ones they had before the divorce.

> "After school, you will get off the bus and come home as usual with the babysitter. If it is my day to see you, I will be home by 6:30. If it is Mom's day, she will pick you up. You will still be able to do lacrosse, basketball, and all of your activities. Of course, you can still have friends over to play. These things will all stay the same."

Kids typically blame themselves when parents break up, and it is essential for this myth to be debunked. Even if one parent is mostly to "blame" for the divorce, it is best not to share that with the kids. That is information they don't need to know.

> "No one is to blame for this divorce. We tried to work it out and it did not work. You kids are the best piece of us, and we are always joined together because of you."

Bring up feelings. Acknowledge that it is normal to sometimes feel sad, worried, or angry when parents are getting divorced. In fact, you may want to tell the kids that, while you may be overly emotional at times, it has nothing to do with them—it is the adjustment to this new life, which is hard on everyone. When kids bring up difficult emotions, listen to them, validate their feelings, and reflect on them. We can't necessarily solve our kids' problems or rid our kids of negative emotions, but we can just be there with them. The emotions will eventually fade away when kids are surrounded with comfort and concern.

> "Sometimes, I feel very confused and worried, but I realize it will not last forever and that it helps to talk to someone about my feelings. Please know that your Mom and I are always available to you—to talk or to help in any way we can. Sometimes, a hug is the best thing to cure a situation. Also, please know that if I seem distracted or upset, it has nothing to do with you. We will get better slowly and learn to live in this new way. The love that I have for you is always and forever there."

The talks do not stop there, check in with your kids at least once a week to see if they want to talk about the divorce or feelings that that may come up.

"LIFE ALWAYS WAITS
FOR SOME CRISIS
TO OCCUR BEFORE
REVEALING ITSELF AT ITS
MOST BRILLIANT."

PAULO COEHLO

Chapter 7
BRAVING DANGEROUS CONVERSATIONS

* * * * * * * * * * * *

*O*ne morning during my junior year of high school, as I was getting ready for school, my mother got a phone call from my sister. As my mother cradled the phone, she stopped in her tracks, and I could feel the air around me pause. I distinctly remember the call my mother made just after she hung up from the first call with my sister. She called her work to let them know she wouldn't be in that day because her daughter had been in "an automobile accident." She said "automobile," not car accident. She was slow and deliberate in her delivery, perhaps in an effort to calm her own nerves. When we arrived at the scene, it hit me how much danger my sister had been in. The car was crumpled like a large, silver tissue. And the police officer pointed to a live wire that had landed inches from the car. He said if it had touched the car, she'd be dead. Dead! I didn't run to get my license right away. In fact, I waited a few months after my birthday had passed. My sister was lucky. I was lucky to have seen that and come to understand the true dangers of driving.

Unfortunately, it often takes a trauma to realize the dangers our children face daily. But if you have established a strong relationship with your child and have talked with her daily about the things that go on in her life and in the world around you, she has a better chance of making smart decisions. And she has a better chance of dealing with the aftermath when she makes bad ones.

Thanks to the efforts of many, our children today are in many ways safer on the road than they have been throughout much of recent history. We have new auto safety features, improved driver's education, and stricter rules, generally, across the nation, and these help our children to be safer on the road. But, ultimately, it's up to our kids how safely they will drive. And the same goes for decisions about drinking, drugs, and other risky behaviors.

Research suggests that kids who have a good relationship with their parents are less likely to engage in risky behaviors and more likely to go to their parents with questions and concerns. So, even if the conversation feels hard, know that it's serving a purpose. Your child may still falter (in fact, you want her to, to some degree). But, when your child stumbles, she will be more likely to come to you for advice if you've been having dangerous conversations for years. And, as she gets older, she will hear you in her head, and you will remain an influencer when she makes those risky decisions.

When it comes to dangerous conversations, talk about the topic abstractly first, and share your own experiences. Then ask questions. Most importantly, listen. Look for any red flags that your child may be experiencing difficulties. Red flags can vary, but typically include behavior changes, dietary changes, changes in routine, physical symptoms (red eyes, weight loss or gain), and friendship changes. Behavioral changes include a drop in grades and/or activities, change in sleep habits, change in interests, withdrawal, hopelessness, cutting behavior, giving away possessions, and being overly secretive. Your tween or teen is changing in many ways, and this is natural, but some behavior may stand out as concerning—trust your gut if you notice any of these red flags.

IMPULSE CONTROL AND DECISION-MAKING

The human brain is not fully developed until early adulthood. Saying this to your kid can come off as annoying or patronizing. However, do explain to your child that his development is in the exact right place for himself. Knowing this can provide relief for kids—-there is comfort in knowing that you are actually supposed to make mistakes, try new things, and forget to be cautious all the time.

Good decision-making is a learned process, and is best done through trial and error. It is our job as parents to offer opportunities for trial and error to our kids. Imagine if you went to driver's education class and the first decision you had to make as a driver was on a highway in a rainstorm behind a truck while you were being tailgated. Your child needs to grow into risky situations and be applauded when he makes good decisions and helped when he makes bad ones.

TAKE THREATS SERIOUSLY

A threat to harm others—whether it comes from your own child or from another—should always be taken at face value. Violent acts rarely happen out of the blue. There is almost always a backstory, and the underlying motivations are important for understanding how to defuse a threat or situation. Typically, the backstory includes feelings of rejection, humiliation, and unresolved conflict. The child tries to take back power the only way he feels he can—through violence. This explanation is simply that—not a justification for violence.

If you are concerned about your child's behavior, approach him about it with a school representative or therapist present, if possible, so you have an extra set of eyes and ears to help interpret the situation. If his behavior is not understood and an alternative solution not put into place, the same threatening behavior will likely continue. Kids who threaten could benefit from coaching to develop healthy coping mechanisms and positive relationships with peers and authority figures.

In addition to watching for threats from your child, make sure to talk with him about any troubling behavior from other kids. If he sees or hears peers making threats to others, he should share that information with you and other adults in authority positions. (Also see conversation starters on "Bullying and Being Bullied" in Chapter 9.)

In Practice:
KIDS IN CRISIS

Kids in crisis don't always display the same symptoms. Common concerns for parents of adolescents include substance abuse and suicide. Trust your gut and pay attention to what's going on. Many adolescents experiment with drugs and alcohol, and while it's best to abstain, some experimentation is normal. Watch for red flags, and talk with your child if you are concerned.

According to the Centers for Disease Control, suicide is a growing risk for teens, rising due to increased levels of depression, higher stress, heavy social media use, and greater feelings of isolation. Between 2007 and 2015, the suicide rate for teen boys increased by 31 percent and the rate doubled for teen girls. If your teen is talking about suicide and making suicidal gestures, take his behavior seriously and seek help from a mental health professional.

RED FLAGS FOR A TEEN IN CRISIS: SUBSTANCE ABUSE

Is your child...

> ...going out with friends more often than before?

> ...secretive about friends or activities?

> ...dropping out of school activities, athletics, or other activities?

> ...getting poor grades?

> ...sleeping all the time?

> ...experiencing difficulty focusing?

...moody more often than not?

...demonstrating paranoia, anxiety, depression, or anger?

...hanging out with different friends?

RED FLAGS FOR A TEEN IN CRISIS: SELF-HARM OR SUICIDE

Is your child...

...often depressed or in what you might describe as an unrelenting funk?

...sleeping much more than usual or much less than usual?

...dealing with a stressful event (loss of someone close, breakup, bullying, friendship change, failure in school)?

...experimenting with drugs and/or alcohol?

...changing in appearance?

...wearing only long sleeves (hiding parts of his body)?

...dropping out of academic/athletic activities?

...giving away possessions?

...obsessed with death?

...less motivated?

So, rather than saying, "No parties ever," how about going slow? If your tween wants to go to a party, call and check if the parent will be home and whether alcohol will be present. Then talk to your child about why you made the call and what his choices are when he gets there if things don't appear as you expect. Walk through a variety of scenarios, and check in after the party to see how it went. Was there anything to be worried about? What decisions did he make? The idea is to set him up for success but to not expect only success.

Help your child understand that developing impulse control is a process. Rather than saying, "You lack impulse control," consider something along the lines of, "Right now it's your job to try new things and practice using impulse control, which you won't completely master right away." Use examples from your own life to illustrate different stages of impulse control. Talking with him directly will show him that his actions have consequences and some can lead to losing your trust. Let your child brainstorm ideas to help him with decision-making (see "Conversation Starters and Prompts," page 136), and also allow him to help decide on appropriate consequences.

PROFIT FROM MISTAKES

To err is not only human, it's necessary for learning. We know this from our own experience, and as tempting as it may be to shelter our children from failure, we need to let them experience disappointment. Failure isn't fun, but it is an important part of the learning process, and is necessary for your child's growth and development. If you expect your kid to make only good decisions, she will end up disappointing you and also herself. She'll be heartbroken because no one can be good all the time, and she'll never figure out how to learn from her mistakes. Research suggests that mistakes aid in the learning process—the only bad mistake is one where no lesson is learned.

Your child is bound to make mistakes in the dangerous category, and you have to hope those will be small mistakes. If you catch your kid doing something dangerous, definitely hold her accountable. Keep in mind that your anger and disappointment will signal the importance of the situation, and there must be a consequence for her actions. But then, maintain a productive attitude, have a conversation, and help her see the bigger picture—help her decide how she can learn from her experience. In other words, if you simply get angrier and angrier or give the silent treatment, you don't offer your child an opportunity for learning. And, while you can hope that her mistakes will be small scale, don't assume that because you have a "good kid" her mistakes won't be big. Good people make mistakes and do bad things.

REFRAIN FROM JUDGMENT

We can't help but judge; it's in our nature. But we can stop ourselves from sharing our judgments with others. When you judge your child, or, worse, his friends, you signal to him that you disapprove. And while you might think that's a good thing because you are, in essence, sharing your values, your critical comments could deter him from confiding in you in the future. Even a mild look of disapproval could stop your child mid-sentence if he has a sense you are passing judgment.

Inspiration

During dangerous conversations:

Honor age-appropriate development.

Learn from mistakes.

Judge sparingly.

Relinquish total control.

Respect independence.

Assume your child has good intentions but stay aware of red flags.

Consider using open-ended questions, and if you're struggling with a response, just listen. If there is an awkward pause, say, "I'm listening—this is very interesting to me." Once your child finishes talking, help him process what he's shared. Rather than simply imposing your values, ask him his opinion. Asking what he thinks will help him to fully form an opinion and begin to develop his own value system and code of ethics. The more supportive you are in this arena, the better prepared your child will be to make independent decisions based on his own judgments and values.

The Dangerous Project
ACTIVITY 1: UNDERSTANDING RISK TAKING AND EMOTIONAL TYPE

As we saw in Chapter 5, there are three basic types of adolescents—exploders, brewers, and stuffers—and knowing which category your kid falls into will help you better understand his approach to risk-taking. If you have not completed the activity to determine your kid's emotional type, please do it now so you can build upon this foundation (see page 95).

Exploders. This type leans toward risk-taking. if your child is the exploder type, he may have a tendency to be a dangerous behavior risk-taker. This type of kid can get easily excited, be caught up in the moment, and fail to consider the consequences of his actions. This type generally does not have much fear of anything, which can put him at risk for getting into trouble. He also seeks approval and sometimes attention from the crowd and may join in activities to gain it.

Build self-awareness with a risk-taker and help him understand his impulses and how they can affect his decisions.

"Remember when you were little and you were not afraid of anything? Do you still feel that way today? In what ways? When we think about drinking, drugs, driving, or sex, how do you think you will handle those situations? Is it sometimes hard for you to say no when other people do something that seems fun, like drinking?"

TEXTING "X"

The "X-plan" offers an out to kids who find themselves in uncomfortable or dangerous situations and want to be picked up. Kids text their parents "X," and the parent then calls the teen's phone and says that there is a family emergency and the parent will pick up the teen. For the X-plan to work well, there should be positive reinforcement for texting "X," as it is a healthy coping skill kids can use to get out of a potentially dangerous situation.

Encourage your risk-taker to think through possible situations before he finds himself faced with them. Come up with a plan for your risk-taker in case he needs a way out of these situations.

Talk through a game plan before your teen is in a dangerous situation. For example, "Let's say you are at a party and people are getting drunk, including the person who gave you a ride. What could you do?" Help your teen brainstorm solutions:

> "How about texting me 'X,' and I will call you and say we have an emergency in the family and I have to pick you up at the party."

Brewers. Kids with this emotional type lean toward being anxious overall, and this tendency plays out in the dangerous behavior category as well. These kids can be overthinkers and may perseverate on negative outcomes. This can cause anxiety and "analysis paralysis," where the kid becomes overwhelmed by her thoughts and therefore is unable to act. Sometimes, these kids need encouragement to attend social functions. Although brewers should appreciate their own thoughtfulness, at times they need to learn how to let things go. They need to learn to recognize previous positive experiences and apply the skills acquired in the past to new experiences. As a parent, recognize the tendency of people with anxiety to participate in excess alcohol consumption.

Walk your brewer through the pros and cons of going to a party.

"What might be fun at this party?"

"Who are the people you like at this party?"

"What would you miss if you did not go?"

"Does anything scare you about this party? What are you worried about?"

Problem-solve with a plan for possible negatives.

"Let's come up with a plan if you get uncomfortable or if people do things that are inappropriate."

Help your brewer develop confidence from past positive experiences.

"When have you done something similar, and it went well? When have you been worried, but you went anyway and had a good experience?"

Address the link of substance abuse and anxiety.

"Just remember that, while your worries may be lessened when drinking or smoking pot, this short-term fix behavior can become addictive and dangerous, and you can end up acting in ways you ordinarily wouldn't. What do you think you can do when you feel anxious at the party? Let's problem solve together."

Stuffers. Kids with this emotional type have a tendency to be joiners in the dangerous behavior category. Stuffers love social activity and enjoy fun. They like everyone to have a good time and will join in activities, for better or worse. Their anxiety comes from a feeling that someone may not like them, and they

SAFE FRIENDS

Safe friends are party buddies that have each other's backs. They have their friends' parents' phone number in case their friend needs a pick-up or is in trouble. This arrangement should be discussed before the party, concert, or other event.

can be talked into doing things because "everyone else is doing it." Because of this need to please, stuffers need lots of information and planning before they are faced with opportunities for risky behavior. They also need some work in developing their own identity and values separate from the group.

Help your teen to envision how he would like the party to go.

"I know you like to have a good time and you are a fun-loving person. I want you to have fun, but also be safe. If you are going to enjoy this party while staying safe, what would have to happen? What can you do to ensure your safety? For example, have a designated driver, name a 'safe friend,' have a parent chauffeur, call an Uber, or text "X" if you need an escape plan."

Emphasize safety.

"If you have had too much to drink, how would you like to handle it? Let's come up with a specific plan."

Talk about identity and values.

"Sometimes, when we're in a group of people, it is easy to forget who we are and how we want to behave. Just because other friends are doing things like drinking, drugs, or sex, this does not mean that you should do these things. You are your own person and can always say no to things that don't seem right to you. If something does not seem right, take a time-out to really think about what is going on before doing something that is really risky. Remember who you are."

ACTIVITY 2: FIND YOUR KID'S NATURAL HIGH

Help your child find her natural high. This feeling of excitement could come through extracurricular activities, hanging out with friends, baking, reading—you name it. The best way to keep out of trouble is to stay busy *and* engaged with other things. This does not mean your child needs to be overscheduled or has to identify her true passion by age sixteen. But it is important that kids have something they enjoy and look forward to. Having interests that they love to pursue will help them understand what it means to be engaged and will help to support them in making healthy choices. Ideally, they will find activities that surround them with people who encourage them and challenge them to set goals and feel fulfilled.

ACTIVITY 3: WHAT'S THE NEWS?

Find a news article or program about something that scares you (a teen driving accident or suicide, for example). Send it to your child to read or watch and tell her that you'd be interested to know what she thinks. This will encourage her to keep up-to-date with the world outside of your home and school, and also shows her that you are thinking about her. If your child brings up the topic, great, and if not, find a moment to refer to it. Ask her what she thought and share your concerns. Then use the conversation starters and prompts that follow to dig deeper.

CONVERSATION STARTERS AND PROMPTS

Here are some prompts and talking points for starting a dangerous conversation with your child:

ALCOHOL AND DRUGS

Before you begin a conversation about alcohol and drugs, think about the personality of your tween/teen (see page 95). Based on your child's personality type, your conversation may be very different, but the message will be the same. Abstinence from alcohol and drugs is the simplest and safest option of all, but not every child will be able to say no to everything at every opportunity. We need to be realistic in our expectations, and to know that—as with sex—teens will be tempted many times in many ways to try alcohol and drugs.

Remember that decision-making is hard and that coming to good decisions consistently is a process. If you tell your child to simply "say no," you are not arming him for a time when he might be tempted to say yes. Share your concerns and the very real dangers that come with drug and alcohol consumption. Don't be afraid to share personal experiences—exposure will not encourage your child to imbibe.

"Have you ever had alcohol or tried any drugs?" (Try to keep this an earnest question and dig deep rather than judge and impose consequences.)

"I worry about you."

"What do you think concerns me most about you drinking or using drugs?"

"Have you been to a party or in a situation where people were drinking alcohol?"

"Do your friends drink? Do you like the idea of it? What excites you or interests you about it?"

ASSAULT AND HARASSMENT

Be clear about defining assault and harassment—these are abuses of power. They can be of a sexual nature, though are not always, and they can look different in different cases. A teacher or doctor can abuse power, and so can a close family friend, a relative, a beloved coach, or a boss (even for a summer job or internship). There are many examples in the media of assault and harassment, and you can use these to start conversations. Use the conversation to elicit thoughts from your son or daughter. Help your child to form his own ideas and perspective on a variety of cases. Compare the cases and look for answers to your child's questions, sharing examples from your own life if you have any.

"Have you ever noticed a friend being treated differently by a teacher or coach? Favored? Left out? Did it seem reasonable?"

"Has anyone ever made you feel uncomfortable in a sexual way? Has anyone made comments or done something to make you feel hurt or scared? What did they do?"

"What was your reaction to this? What did you want to do? If you could go back in time, what do you think your reaction should have been? Do you think you should tell anyone else about it?"

"Have you ever noticed situations that seemed unfair? What do you think makes the difference between a fair exchange and one that is unfair?"

"Have you ever felt bullied in a situation and been too embarrassed to say anything?"

"Why do you think people are afraid or embarrassed to speak up in these cases?"

"What do you think you would do if you saw someone being harassed?"

Teens will sometimes cut themselves as a coping mechanism for stress and emotional pain. Cutting externalizes internal pain and the body responds by surging with natural opiates to help deal with the pain, creating a feeling of relief in the body. This desire to feel relief from internal pain and to represent that pain is the main reason teens engage in this behavior. Teens engaging in cutting need to develop healthier coping strategies for dealing with stress, such as talking with trusted adults and friends, getting support (therapy), exercise, journaling, and refocusing their thoughts through healthier actvities. Broach the subject with them directly if you think there may be a problem.

"I noticed the marks on your arm [or insert the physical signs you notice]. What's going on?"

State what you know. "Sweetheart, I see that you cut your arm."

Reach out. "Can we talk about this? I want to understand what is going on."

Reassure. "I want to understand and help you. You can tell me anything. I am always here for you."

DRIVING

Driving is a major rite of passage for teenagers—and also a dangerous responsibility we give kids before their brains are fully developed. As with any skill, practice makes perfect, and one of the benefits of teaching your teen to drive is that she is with you and you have some control over the situation while she learns. Of course, one natural disadvantage is that teens are young and fearless.

Hopefully, you feel prepared and well-supported in your instruction (and perhaps you've even enrolled your child in a driving class). In addition to teaching the rules of the road and basic driving and maneuvering skills, offer your child your perspective on the act of driving and on her safety.

And, while drinking and driving is a very real danger, it's not the only one to be worried about and prepared for. Texting, distraction from other passengers, and lack of sleep are real and growing concerns for all drivers, especially teens. Stress that your concern and nervousness is not a sign that you lack trust but due to the seriousness of the situation. Remember that getting her license doesn't mean that your child is ready to drive everywhere on her own, and it definitely doesn't mean she is ready to drive under every possible circumstance. Even you get thrown off by a little black ice, right? Be very clear with your child that a license is one step of earning the responsibility to drive.

> "You need to have a minimum seven hours of sleep before driving—how can we set up our routine so you can have that? What are your options when you haven't had that much sleep?"

> "What are the requirements/limitation of devices in the car, including GPS?"

> "Who are you legally allowed to have in the car while you drive? Who do you think is appropriate to have in the car while you drive?"

> "Let's practice saying no to getting in a car."

> "What options do we have to get you to and from various places so I don't have to worry you will drive drunk or get in someone else's car if you have been drinking?"

> "If you have been drinking and you need to get somewhere, what are your choices?"

> "Who can you call if you don't want to call me?"

> "I'd rather you find somewhere safe to be than have you home by curfew, and I'd rather have you disappoint me than have you in danger."

Not all dangerous behaviors seem like a big problem upon first glance. Minor vices deserve just as much attention as the headline-grabbing issues facing tweens and teens.

Recent research shows a growing problem with addiction to mobile devices for kids and adults. Observe your child's use (and possibly overuse) of her device(s) and check in about any concerns. Set aside screen-free time for family and for your child to be with her peers. It's a great idea to make meals a time for face-to-face interaction, so try putting the phones away for family dinner.

"I'd like to set some time aside where we are all off our phones—what are good times of day for us to disconnect?"

"Is there a day we could set aside to be free of our screens and just have fun together?" Start with a few hours; it doesn't have to be a regular occurrence right away.

Vaping is shown to lead to cigarette smoking and addiction. It's a new fad that is being heavily marketed to young people, and the devices are easily accessible.

"Do kids at school vape?"

"What do you think about it?"

"What do you think makes it cool?"

"Have you ever tried vaping? Do you think you would?"

SUICIDE

People worry that talking about suicide will inspire their children to consider it. This is not the case. Talking about it—in an honest and serious way—can be very helpful for kids. And, if you have concerns that your child is considering suicide, seek help immediately. We have included national organizations in the Suggested Resources section (see page 194), and you can refer to them for general help or to be steered to local support. Also, see the conversation starters on mental health in Chapter 9.

"Have you ever felt that kind of 'inside' pain that you worried would never go away? Have you ever known anyone who felt like they wanted to hurt themselves?"

"How do you handle pain? Fear?"

"Do you feel like you have options? Do you want my help thinking through others?"

Help your child identify a safe adult to confide in and emphasize how important it is to tell someone immediately if he is thinking of harming himself.

"How are you feeling talking about this? It is normal to feel uncomfortable talking about suicide, but it is very important that you know my door is always open for you to tell me any feelings that you are having. Let's talk again in a few days."

This is a good start to get the conversation going, but don't stop there. Continue to check in with your child's feelings about the subject. By doing this, you are establishing yourself as a safe place to talk and explore the entire rainbow of feelings that kids experience.

CONVERSATION IN ACTION

You notice that your sixteen-year-old son is tearful and staring intently at his phone. He tells you that he found out through social media that a student at his high school committed suicide. His friends are posting "RIP" to Snapchat and sharing stories and rumors about this incident. You take a look at your son's phone and realize that this story is going viral. How do you handle this situation?

The first thing to do is check with the school and trusted friends about the truth of this story. In this case, it was true—a high school student struggling with gender identity took his life. Second, encourage your son to take a break from the phone for a bit to process and debrief this very disturbing incident. Remember that in a crisis, there is an opportunity to learn. As parents, we have an opportunity to model ways to deal with emotionally sensitive issues.

Open up the conversation with your son. It is important to dispel rumors and stories as soon as possible. Put all technology away, sit close, and make eye contact—this is a difficult conversation. Remember that it is okay for you to cry and become upset. That is a normal reaction to such a sad situation. In addition, use your "gut instinct" to check in with your child as the conversation continues—some kids might do best if this tough conversation takes place over a few days, while other kids might respond better if you sit down and hash it out all at once. Remember, the point of the conversation is to help your child process the information and come up with a plan of action if he is very sad and/or worried about hurting himself or if he has a friend who is very sad and/or is talking about hurting himself.

One common misconception is that talking about suicide inspires kids to commit suicide, and this is simply not true. The more you talk in a healthy fashion, the more your child will learn to process his own feelings and come to you and other trusted adults with problems.

Start the conversation with empathy and compassion.

"It's normal to become upset and distressed when you hear of disturbing situations. It's very sad to know that someone was hurting so much that he hurt himself."

"I know this is hard to understand and make sense of. Even as adults, we can't really understand why someone would do this. Let's talk about our worries and concerns together and figure out a plan for what to do if you hear a friend talking about wanting to hurt himself or if you feel very sad."

Then start with some basic facts about the individual case, if you are responding to a specific incident. You may only get through part of what you'd planned to say before the conversation takes a turn, and you may not anticipate the turns it will take. Your son may be very interested in the facts, might start to wonder about his own concerns, or might relate the event to other friends or family.

> "I found out today that a boy in our town committed suicide last night—this means that he killed himself. I don't know him personally so I don't know the reasons why, but it hurts my heart to know that anyone felt that sad and alone. I wish I could have helped him."

> "There will be lots of rumors and people wanting to make this situation very dramatic, and we don't want to be a part of that. Please come to me with anything that you hear or see that is upsetting or doesn't seem right. Some kids can post upsetting things, and you have to realize that much of it is probably not true, that they are doing this for attention."

Then it is time to open up the discussion:

"What have you heard about this incident so far?"

"What are some of the feelings you have about this?"

"What are your concerns about this?"

Remember, some people feel numb when they hear of suicide, so feeling "frozen" is a normal reaction as well. Next, start talking about a plan of action. Children and adults feel better when they recognize that they have the power to do some good and help someone else or themselves.

"Has a friend ever talked to you about hurting himself?"

"What did you do about it?"

"Was that the right thing to do?"

"What else could you do?"

Reiterate that talking about hurting yourself is a serious thing, and sometimes children are in severe pain and need immediate help. Whenever kids witness another child talk about hurting himself, they need to tell a trustworthy adult like a teacher, counselor, principal, or parent. They may be saving the child's life by getting him the help he needs. And your child can come to you even if he's not sure if it's a real threat or problem. Better safe than sorry.

Then turn the discussion to your child/children. Here are some questions you can ask:

"Have you felt sad or depressed?"

"Have you ever felt like hurting yourself?"

"During this time, what did your body feel like?"

"What thoughts were going through your mind?"

"Did you have worries or sadness that you felt might never end?"

"What helped to make you feel better?"

"What else would help the pain go away?"

Emotional pain is extraordinarily difficult to talk about, and the fact that you are even asking these questions and opening up a conversation about suicide is powerful. As parents, we can't always expect much of a response from our children. The most important thing you can do is let your child know that you are open to discussing all types of emotions, including pain, depression, and desperate sadness.

Always make it clear with children that any emotional pain is temporary, but killing yourself is permanent. Like a broken bone, emotional pain may need treatment for healing, but, with the right care, healing can happen. By talking about things that hurt, we connect and build a stronger, healthier connection to our children and our community.

"CHARACTER CANNOT BE DEVELOPED IN EASE AND QUIET."

HELLEN KELLER

Chapter 8

NURTURING CHARACTER CONVERSATIONS

*O*ne snowy December evening, in my rush to get last-minute gifts for the holidays, drive the kids to their various extracurricular activities, and get dinner on the table, I turned the wrong way on a street. I pulled into a parking lot to turn myself around, stopped for a car ahead of me, and then heard a horn and felt a bump. Just what I needed—an accident. I pulled over and got out to exchange information with the driver. He refused to roll down the window, pulled around my car, and sped off to the other side of the lot. I was at a loss. I could have left but I wasn't sure if he was over it and just parking or if he wanted to talk, so I pulled up next to him and tried again.

He wouldn't get out of his car, and I stood there, in the snow, asking if he wanted to talk. He eventually rolled down his window to yell at me and accused me of backing into his car. I stayed calm, asked him if he wanted to inspect the cars—there was no apparent damage—and, eventually, we exchanged insurance information. I offered my hand to shake and wished him a happy holiday season, at which point he looked up and thanked me for staying so calm. He went on to apologize for his behavior and we parted in good terms, connecting the next day to confirm that no significant damage had been done.

A mild story in the end, but throughout the experience my emotions had soared and plummeted. I shared this with my family at dinner, and the most remarkable part to me was that, in the midst of the incident, this man was able to recognize his bad behavior, own it, and make things right. Even though this man had made a bad decision by refusing to engage and then losing his temper (which we all are guilty of), in the end, he demonstrated strong character.

Character is the collage of decisions and actions our children make—our job is to help them eventually make good decisions independent of our input (and when we're not looking). If you consider that you are raising your children in the here and now with the goal of preparing them to live on their own, you can see the benefit of scaffolding decision-making as kids grow: It's sensible to make decisions for kids when they are very young; to make decisions with them as they begin to develop their capacity for judgment; and then simply to weigh in when they are able to make decisions on their own.

We can't expect more of our kids than they can give us, so they need to know they are loved and nurtured as they are. And while we can hope to teach them to be "good people," we also have to allow for the beauty of imperfection and educate them that good people don't always do good things. In other words, you can be good, kind, and loving and still have feelings of anger, frustration, and jealousy. This is what makes us human, and we shouldn't shame our children for having or expressing such feelings.

DECISION-MAKING

Having a strong character doesn't mean always making good decisions, but it does mean taking responsibility for our decisions and how our words and actions communicate to others. Through conversations with your children, you can reaffirm your love, your hopes, your expectations, and also your understanding and compassion for who they truly are. Kids will develop character through your encouragement, and also through your discipline. You can use conversations to help them better understand who they are on their journey to developing character. Point to examples, and teach by your own behavior, good and bad.

Actions speak louder than words—it's an old adage but worth reminding ourselves because it holds true for ourselves and our children. We may say we believe something, but do we stay true to our beliefs, our morals, and our values when difficult situations arise? Point to examples where you have upheld your deeply held beliefs and to instances when you haven't, and help your child see the differences. Teaching strong character is not about acting unfailingly in a noble and honorable way, but rather about making every effort to do what is right and learning from the experience when you don't. Opportunities for teaching character can be as simple as pointing out when you've been given more change than you should have received at the store and as complicated as dealing with the aftermath of your child bullying another child at school.

MORALS AND VALUES

When our children are young they mimic us in many ways, and that includes adopting our morals and values. They tend to develop their own principles, usually rooted in yours, as they are exposed to the world in bigger ways and to friendships outside the home. Share your values and stand by them. Talk to your child when you stand strong for something you believe in and when you feel like you should have but didn't for one reason or another. Encourage your child to advocate for his beliefs, even if he chooses to support something you do not.

As kids enter adolescence (and sometimes just before), they might push back on some of the ideals you hold fast to. And this might hurt you. Keep in mind that such pushback is their job, and that it is a good thing they must ultimately develop their own principles. It's your job to offer feedback in a constructive manner and to let your children experiment. So when you and your child are in conflict over a belief or value, ask yourself if it's worth it. What is the goal of the argument? Will arguing help the situation? Are you helping your child develop on his own? Use your conversations with your child to talk through decisions (yours and his) and keep an open mind. Reassure your child that these decisions, little and large, are the ones that help to shape his character.

I cannot tell you how many times I have sat in a parent-teacher conference as the teacher and heard variations of, "Am I in the right conference?" or, "You must be talking about some other student." It's often said, at least in part, as a joke. And I have uttered the same words as a parent. My child, modest? My child, looking for an academic challenge? But there is much truth in the observation. Our children are different at home and at school. It's natural for them to want to make a positive impression around their peers and to please their teachers or other adult influencers in their lives. They wear different hats and usually know where they can take one off. And, on the flip side, they sometimes act out for attention when they know better. They are constantly building character as they process situations, make choices in response to the situations, and reflect on and/or evaluate the reaction they get.

Consider yourself a guide or facilitator as your child enters the tween and teen years. Whereas before you may have been more of a manager or director, you are now one influencer among many—and you want to maintain that influence. Ask questions and listen to understand your child's reasoning. Support good decisions and ask your child to judge poor ones rather than judging them yourself.

Tweens and teens are naturally self-centered, lacking developed decision-making skills (executive functioning), and often starving for attention from their peers. In the information age, they are forced to develop character both on- and offline. Given the capacity to broadcast through a smartphone, the potential for disaster is substantial. A phone allows kids to post sexy or otherwise inappropriate thoughts, pictures, and ideas on a whim. These can be easily duplicated and shared no matter how private they may feel. The lack of face-to-face interaction hides the teen from an immediate negative reaction, such as humiliation, and provides an outlet for gaining the attention he so desires.

The problem is that a teen does not necessarily realize how others may view his actions or understand that a comment or photo may be shared all over the school and beyond, damaging his reputation. The thought of consequences is not in the forefront of the teen's brain, because executive functioning is not yet fully developed. As parents, we need to remind our teens often that the material we post online, or share via text or apps, has consequences. This applies not only to sexting but to other actions as well. For example, consider the June 2017 story of ten Harvard students who had their admission rescinded after sharing inappropriate memes and messages in a private Facebook group. Adding some scary stories of your own can help get the point across more clearly. If your teen is posting inappropriate things online, start the conversation with an understanding that your kid ended up in this position because of his brain's immaturity and his lack of inexperience, and educate him about his own brain and body.

In Practice: SCREEN TIME

Offering opportunities for developing independence is important for tweens and teens so that they can learn firsthand what it means to live with their decisions and accept responsibility for them. These opportunities can include social media. While the number of hours dedicated to screen time for both schoolwork and socializing has dramatically increased over the years, the way kids relate to others is also different from the way we did as kids. This isn't all bad. There are many more opportunities to meet or stay in touch with kids who are not local, and there are more ways for kids who don't naturally socialize in traditional ways to engage with others via a facilitated route (for example, with gaming or chatting).

While you want to encourage face-to-face connections, also support your child's online engagement. With young children or kids being newly introduced to digital devices, monitor their online activity very strictly. Watch just about all they do for a set period of time. Talk to them about the importance of getting to know the platform or app they are using and the importance of handling that tool carefully. By looking at every interaction you cue to your kids that this is important enough that you're taking the time to do it, and that what they post is worth noting.

Be a part of your children's digital lives, in appropriate ways. Remember, your parents didn't know everything you did as a kid, so as your tween and teen develops more maturity and demonstrates responsibility online, back off from checking frequently and do more check-ins together. Talk about what you're looking for and why. Ask your kids to share some of what they're doing on their devices rather than simply policing their activity.

MINDFULNESS—AND WHAT IT MEANS

How we deal with stress says a lot about our character and values. If we parents scream in distress and bring our exhausting workday home with us, we teach our kids that, when life is stressful, it is okay to take out our frustrations on other people. In other words, we distribute instead of diffusing our stress.

One of the best tools to combat stress is mindfulness. Mindfulness is simply paying attention to the present moment. Neuroscientific research suggests that mindfulness helps to boost resiliency and develops new neural pathways in the brain. In other words, mindfulness helps us develop new road maps for dealing with life's stressors. As humans, we tend to spend much of our time either "future forecasting" or reliving the past. Often, this forecasting and reliving involves mostly negative possibilities and experiences that our brain tries to figure out. What about focusing on the here and now—the present moment? This is mindfulness, bringing our attention back to the present moment, to what is happening and where we are now.

Research suggests that incorporating mindfulness into your parenting is beneficial for both you and your children. A calm, less judgmental, and non-reactive approach is associated with parenting practices that encourage more positive behavior and engagement in children. Mindfulness is about being present in the moment and understanding what you have control over and what your own choices are; it's not about "being positive" and trying to spin the situation.

Use mindfulness to approach self-awareness and actions. For example, developing a healthy body awareness is a challenge for most adolescents. As our children develop, their awareness of their bodies changes as well. The rush of hormones, acne, rapid weight gain, and mood swings can take over even the most well-adjusted teen. In your conversations with your child, talk about taking care of yourself mindfully. This means accepting the current situation nonjudgmentally, recognizing that everything is temporary (nonattachment), and taking care of yourself in the present moment.

As adolescents develop, their bodies can feel like a battlefield. Both boys and girls have impossibly high standards for what they are "supposed" to look like, and often they are disappointed that their bodies are not like those of the people they pattern themselves after, often models, actors, or professional athletes. Social media certainly plays a large role in kids' developing sense of self, but as a parent you also have the ability to be a major influencer. It helps to open body image conversations with your teen with the understanding that her struggle with who she is and how she wants to be perceived is real. Acknowledge that body image can sometimes be an issue, and ask your child what she thinks. You can also reinforce the importance of health and strength, and can model that you believe what you say through your own words and actions.

PRACTICE GRATITUDE

Teach your child gratitude. Gratitude helps kids develop empathy and also protects them from constantly comparing their lives with others'. These days, you can instantly see via social media everything someone else is doing, buying, enjoying, and so on. By stopping to acknowledge what you have in life (both tangible and otherwise), you develop a deeper appreciation for your life.

A true practice of gratitude implies that you express appreciation on a regular basis. It can be as easy as keeping a journal, sharing gratitude at a family meal, or sending thank-you notes. No matter how you choose to express gratitude, help your child understand its importance and make it a regular habit. A fun way to start a conversation is to share the things you are grateful for and ask your kids to share theirs at the dinner table, then ask questions about their thoughts.

Remind your child that character development is a process and her actions demonstrate her character in the moment. Her character is who she is at her very heart. Help her to be her own person by identifying and celebrating the best of her character. Focus on the positive, but don't ignore challenges. For example, it's okay to have high expectations for winning a game or getting good grades, but be sure your child knows that it is her integrity as she participates that defines who she is. The result (whether she wins or loses a game or aces or bombs a test) is simply a measure of how much she can do in that moment. Who she is can affect how she does next time. To say "winning isn't everything" is fine—but show her how her character helps her win in the long term.

Assess the ways in which you offer your child opportunities to help her build character. As you look through this list of ideas, consider what you're already doing and what you could do more of.

Chores. Does your child have regular chores around the house? Are there more or different ones she could take on? Doing chores helps a child understand familial responsibility and develop a sense of pride for her home. Talk with your child about what chores would be most helpful and offer choice if you can.

Homework. Does your child do his own homework every night, independent of your help? If you do offer a lot of support, can you start to pull back? Think of homework as a communication tool between your child and his teacher. It should be an authentic account of what your child is capable of. If your child is struggling, be sure to include the teacher in the conversation about how you are participating or what help you can arrange.

Volunteering. Does your child do any regular or periodic volunteering? Volunteering can help your child develop empathy and a sense of appreciation. This helps to combat those feelings of want that often plague adolescents.

Charitable giving. As a family, do you donate to any organizations or efforts? Is there one you could identify with your child to support?

Job. Does your tween or teen have a job? Jobs help kids develop responsibility outside the home and learn many real-life skills. Encourage your kid to put up flyers for babysitting, pet sitting, yardwork, or other tasks.

If your child is old enough to apply for a job in a business, support that effort. And encourage kids to save their income for something special.

Extracurricular activities. Is there an area of interest your child could explore in a deeper way? It's great for kids to take part in activities outside academics if they have the interest and time and it's in your budget. You may be able to take advantage of inexpensive or free offerings through your town or city. The important thing is to focus on what they learned through participation (for example, practicing an instrument) and not on the outcome (for instance, winning a championship).

Responsibility for siblings. Does your child watch younger siblings or behave for older siblings? Are your children kind and helpful to one another? Talk about ways they can engage with one another and offer them opportunities to watch each other. If one is in charge, make sure the other is responsible for something.

Spirituality and gratitude. How does your child show gratitude? Do you have rituals that you could add into your everyday life to increase your child's connection to spirituality? Do you have rituals that you could add that would increase your child's level of gratitude? Could you add more tech-free relaxation, like walking in nature, gardening, yoga, meditation, and art that stimulate a grounded, quietness in the brain?

Inspiration

During character conversations. . .

Encourage decision making and acknowledge the choices.

Follow through with consequences.

Honor your child's developing morals and values.

Be mindful in the moment and know that this, too, shall pass.

Develop a practice of gratitude and true appreciation.

The Character Project

ACTIVITY 1: SHARE A LESSON

Share with your child something you did that you're not proud of. Be sure to include the consequences or ramifications you experienced. Talk about how you felt. Why are you not proud? Explain what you learned, and, if applicable, how you used that lesson for a future decision you made. Then share with your child a time you did something you were proud of, big or small. What inspired you to make the decision? Was it natural or did it take convincing or consideration? What were the outcomes? Why are you proud?

ACTIVITY 2: PRACTICE MINDFULNESS

One of the easiest ways to practice mindfulness is through breath control. Breath control is a great tool because it is always available. Read through this section with your child before beginning, so you can give yourself fully to the experience.

Sit comfortably with your child. Situate yourself with cushions, and close your eyes. Put one hand on your belly and observe the characteristics of your breath. Your breath will change, sometimes becoming deeper and sometimes shallower. Feel your breath start in your belly and work its way up to your mouth and nose. Think of the breath like a wave cresting on the shore, lapping in and out. Try to stay focused on just the breath, as your mind might wander. Then broaden your focus to the details of your experience—your five senses at the present—touch, smell, taste, sight, and hearing. When you feel yourself begin to lose focus, gently bring yourself back to the present.

If you're struggling with this or want to extend the practice, consider downloading a sample guided meditation. Customize a meditation for yourself and for your child. Think of a favorite place and create the sensory experience. Consider asking your kid to create a customized meditation for herself.

ACTIVITY 3: BODY TALK

Talk with your child about body image. This is an issue for both girls and boys. While sitting with your child and watching TV or scrolling through social media, ask your child what he thinks about the images, bodies, and messages being portrayed. Encourage him to become an independent thinker and to look at images and messages at an arm's length, rather than being manipulated by advertising or someone else's agenda. Talk about realistic expectations for one's body.

You can also talk about how the "ideal" body has changed over time and is different in different parts of the world. Look to ancient and classical art, turn-of-the-century pictures, and older movies. Ideas about the perfect body have changed even within my lifetime—growing up in the 1980s, thin was in, but now the booty is back and a wider range of bodies are considered beautiful. Men don't have to have a six-pack stomach to be attractive or appealing. Discuss who your child is trying to please, and how that changes how he feels. Note that advertisers prey on teens' insecurities, so it is important to talk and support your teen with some healthy body image.

SUPPORTING YOUR CHILD'S SELF-IMAGE

Focus on character. When you talk with your child, focus on who she is as a person rather than her accomplishments or appearance.

Celebrate diversity. Enjoy a variety of people and activities in your life, showing that there is no one norm to aspire to.

Talk about decision-making. When your child makes a choice, talk about the intention and how it led to the outcome rather than focusing only on the outcome (or possible punishment).

Provide opportunities to promote independence. Allow your child small freedoms so she learns that she can depend on herself.

Encourage teens to talk about the activities that make their bodies feel good and that they find pleasurable. Provide your teen with some examples that you personally have established for your own self-care plan. Some examples include taking a bath, doing yoga, exercising, making and eating a nourishing meal, sitting in the sun, going swimming, being out in nature, or even riding roller-coasters or other thrill rides, for the adrenaline junkies.

Help your child choose at least one activity that helps him feel good and commit to it each week for the next month. Put it on the calendar, and help him experience self-care. If you are not able to join your teen in his activities, be sure to check in about his self-care experience. Ask your kid, "What did you do? How did it make you feel? How did your body feel? Did you feel any different afterward? Is this something you would like to do on a regular basis?" Find a few different self-care rituals for your teen to add into his routine. Your homework is to model for your child your own self-care routines. Kids are most likely to repeat what they see.

CONVERSATION STARTERS

Here are some prompts and talking points for starting a character conversation with your child:

ACTIONS AND BEHAVIOR

Understand that your child will sometimes make poor choices. Celebrate the good choices and learn from the not-so-good ones. While it's appropriate to enforce consequences and be consistent about them, don't overlook the opportunity to discuss issues and make use of the lessons learned.

When a problem or a crisis (whether minor or major) arises, ask questions first and try to understand the story before making assumptions.

"What happened? What inspired you to do that? Who else was involved? Why do you think I'm surprised/disappointed? How do you feel about what happened?"

Then make a plan together about what should follow.

"What do you think we should do about this?"

"Who else needs to be involved?"

Praise effort. Achievement is great, and it's good to celebrate it, but note the importance of the effort involved. And when effort doesn't lead to achievement, continue to stress the importance of effort.

"You've practiced a lot, and I am sorry you lost the game. But your practice is paying off. I could tell by your [insert a positive change in your child]."

"What do you think you should focus your practice on? Have you talked to your coach about where to focus your practice?"

Try to encourage learning for the sake of learning rather than for a grade or other payoff.

"What are you learning these days? How does it relate to your experience?"

If your child is struggling in a class or is simply disinterested, talk about how the subject relates to the real world. What applications can you imagine? If you're struggling to find those connections, investigate.

"I know it's hard to work at something that doesn't seem relevant. Can you think of any way this might help you in the future?"

"Who uses the information you're learning on a regular basis?"

"Would you like to connect with someone [insert the name of a person if you know of anyone] to talk about how this is important in the bigger picture?"

When your child receives a grade, it's good to express excitement over what went into the grade or comfort her disappointment if she is unhappy with the grade.

"I'm proud of how hard you worked on that project. How do you feel about it?"

"Can you tell me about your grade? Is there something you're struggling with? Is there anything I can do to help you? Do you want to talk to your teacher or counselor? Is there someone else you (or we) can go to?"

Stress the importance of grades and achievement as part of the process of learning. Grades communicate what your child knows, doesn't know, or is learning. These should be seen as guideposts more than summary statements of your child's worth.

"It feels like we're rushing around a lot lately. Do you have the time you need?" If the answer is no: "What can we do to ease up on our schedule a bit?"

"Do you feel like you have the support you need?" If the answer is no: "What kind of support do you think you need? Where do you think we should go first for help?"

HEALTHY HABITS

Focus on strength and character more than outer appearance. Be careful how you talk about your own appearance and critiques. Support independent style and celebrate uniqueness.

"What makes someone beautiful? What do you think is meant by 'It's what's on the inside that counts'?"

"What makes you special? What do you think I love about you?"

Encourage healthy eating and fitness. Invite your child to participate in physical activities: a hike, a fitness class, a game of H.O.R.S.E. at the local park, a 5K race to support a cause you both care about, or just a fun day at the beach.

Include your child in food decisions and maybe in food preparation if he is interested.

"What do you want to have for dinner? Can you start dinner today?"

"What are you eating at school? Do you want to prepare your own lunches? Is there anything we can keep in the house that you'd prefer?"

HUMILITY

There is a fine line between being proud and being a braggart and also between being humble and being passive. Celebrate success and effort, and encourage your child to do so as well. Talk about what she says and model appropriate expressions.

"What are you proud of? Why?"

"Will you share that with your friends?"

Discuss success in your life with pride.

"Did I ever tell you about the time I...?"

"Have you ever felt that way?"

Point to examples that demonstrate bragging and talk about options.

"I can see that the way the other team celebrated upset you and your teammates. Do you think you would have reacted the same way if you had won?"

IDENTITY

Talk about family history. Who are you like? What family members inspired you? Disgusted you? Why? How did their actions or the way they made you feel change who you are?

"How would you describe yourself?"

"What makes you, you?"

"What, if anything, would you change about yourself?"

Set high expectations of integrity and be okay if your child does not always meet them. Consider sharing a time when you demonstrated great integrity and a time when you didn't. What did you learn from each experience and how did the experience impact your actions moving forward? What have you tried to repeat and what have you tried to change?

"When have you felt compromised?"

"Are you trying your hardest in school?"

"Have you ever felt the need to push harder than you can?"

"What do you consider cheating? Are there times when you think it's okay to cheat or lie? Has there ever been a time you felt like cheating? What did you do?"

"Thank you for trying so hard. Where do you think you went wrong?"

"I love you, and that's why this is so disheartening to me, but I'm not giving up. What do you think we can do next?"

"Why is _____ important to you? What would you be willing to do to support it/them?"

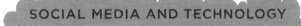

SOCIAL MEDIA AND TECHNOLOGY

As with many things, practice makes perfect. Even with the best instruction, you still need practice to be a good driver, tennis player, or pianist. Introduce social media slowly and enjoy it together at first. Even when your child uses it independently, check in frequently and talk about his interactions.

"What does she mean by that post? Is that a typical thing you see on Instagram?"

"What kinds of posts are you making? Is there anything I can't view? Is there anything I should know about that you might prefer not to tell me?"

MANAGING SOCIAL MEDIA METRIC ANXIETY

It's normal for a teen to want to be liked, and lack of attention can cause feelings of isolation or depression. Teens today face a phenomenon that builds on this feeling of rejection, a phenomenon that we couldn't even imagine a few years ago. With social media, kids can see instantaneously if people like or laugh at their posts. They attreact followers and follow other people. This can help build connections, but can also leave kids feeling left out or rejected. Lack of response and few followers can lead to feelings of low self-worth. For example, imagine your daughter posts a picture of herself singing and no one likes it. It could be no one saw it or no one understood how much it meant to her. Whatever the case, she could internalize the lack of reactions and assume people think she is a bad singer. Here are four ways to help if your child is dealing with Social Media Metric Anxiety.

1. **Teach and model self-regulation.** Help your child learn ways to reduce screen time that causes anxiety, such as setting alarms, limiting devices during certain times of day, or planning other activities.

2. **Identify problem areas.** Are there certain apps, people, or situations that cause more anxiety than others? If so, name them and help your child to see the issues.

3. **Try alternate activities.** Find or rediscover activities that your child enjoys and encourage her to pursue them. These can be both on- and offline.

4. **Keep the big picture in mind.** Help your child understand that this is only one piece of growing up and that feedback on social media does not dictate who she is.

Spirituality can mean different things to different people. For some, it can include nonreligious practices such as meditation, yoga, and mindfulness. A walk in the woods or time at the beach can feel spiritual. Whatever your spiritual practice is, honor it and share it with your child. What makes you feel anchored or how does it lift you? Sometimes, this includes religious traditions. Invite your child to share in your religious and/or spiritual beliefs and practices rather than dictating her participation. This will help her develop her own ideas and beliefs. Be open to other celebrations and ways to honor spirituality that resonate with your child.

"Would you like to join me for a service?"

"What would you prefer to do?"

"What do you enjoy about services? Is there anything you don't enjoy?"

"How would you define your own spirituality?"

"What are ways you feel spiritual?"

"Do your friends have other ideas around spirituality?"

"Is there anything you want to explore or ways that I can support your practice?"

CONVERSATION IN ACTION

You check your son's computer and see an exchange on social media in which he is talking about another classmate in a nasty way, using foul language, and making fun of the other child's appearance and intelligence. You check his texts as part of your agreement about his mobile device use, and he is aware that you sometimes look. However, you do have a sense of guilt that you've invaded his privacy and learned something you weren't meant to know. You ask yourself how he could not have realized you would see this. And how could he be so mean? You've talked about transparency. You've talked about how what teens write will be there forever. You stew during the day, trying to focus on work, but mostly just wait for him to come home from school so you can discuss this.

First of all, take a deep breath. While what you write online can be permanent, there is no guarantee that this hurtful post will get into the hands of the child who is being made fun of. It is natural to be disappointed in your son, but a bad decision or a mean comment doesn't make your child bad or mean. It simply shows that this is an area for growth and learning. Remember that part of standing by your child is standing by him while he accepts responsibility for his actions. Try giving it some time so you can process the situation and so he can transition home and do what needs doing. Find a good time for your conversation, then be open-minded, allow him to respond, and truly listen to him.

Try starting with, "What is your homework situation this evening? I have something serious I want to discuss with you, and I would like to set some time aside when you can talk with me."

If he asks, as kids often do, if he's in trouble or what the conversation is about, respond honestly and directly: "I found something on your computer that concerned me."

This will allow him to process what you will talk about and prepare for the chat, if he needs to. It's best that neither of you enters the conversation overcharged with emotion or on the offense or defense. You're letting him know that you found something, you're concerned, and you want his input.

Once you've established a good time to talk, find a comfortable setting with some privacy. Start with one fact and then lead with questions.

> "I saw something on your computer (say exactly what you found). Can you tell me about it?" Let him respond. Give him time, and allow for quiet if he's not ready.

He tells you that it was a joke, and that this kid is super annoying in class and he and his friends just talk about the kid to be funny. He assures you it's in a private chat group and this is not a big deal at all. His friends post way worse stuff.

Follow up by validating his points and feelings. Validation doesn't mean approval, but it shows you understand his perspective and you're willing to talk through this. Show him you understand that he doesn't think it's such a big deal, but that if it struck you this way, can he imagine how others who are more personally connected might feel?

> "I understand that he's annoying, and it might feel private to you, but nothing you put down in writing on the Internet can be 100 percent safe. This could fall into unintended hands. This is an issue we need to deal with."

Inquire about his motivation. Brainstorm other options for the future.

> "What were you hoping to achieve by saying these things? Did it make you feel good? What else could you have done? What would you do moving forward, ideally?"

This last question signals to your son that you understand he wants to do a good job and he may, in fact, falter again in this same area, but having a plan in place can help.

Ask him for suggestions for making this right now and moving forward. Does he think the other boy needs to know about this? Should he apologize to his friends for his negativity? It's definitely easier to delete the chat and move on, but will he learn from that? What can he do to learn from this situation?

> "What do you think you should do about this?" Listen to his answer and, if possible, set his plan in place, or at least one that he buys into. Maybe try role-playing with him to practice what he will say to whomever he talks to about this.

> "Do you need help? Can you do this? Will you do this?"

Your son needs to know that you're there for him and you will love him in spite of poor decision making. And asking him to generate ways to make good on the situation demonstrates that you know he can take responsibility. Think of yourself as the support and of your son as the problem-solver.

"COURAGE STARTS
WITH SHOWING UP
AND LETTING
OURSELVES BE SEEN."

BRENÉ BROWN

Chapter 9:
FOSTERING BRAVE CONVERSATIONS

* * * * * * * * * * * *

*M*y friend Susan's daughter, Shelly, was shocked one morning when, upon arriving at school, friends gathered around her to say, "I'm so sorry—how are you doing?" At that point, Shelly didn't understand what kind of horror had happened overnight on social media. It turns out her ex-boyfriend had posted a naked picture of her and shared it. Shelly felt ashamed and publicly humiliated, and the conversations that ensued with her mother, the school administration, and the police were terribly upsetting. On top of that, she dealt with the pain of being exposed both so publicly and to her family.

Susan also dealt with a profound shock from the situation. She was forced to recognize that her daughter had posed for these revealing photos and likely had a more intimate relationship than Susan had realized. It took courage for Susan to face this head-on, but she showed Shelly that, no matter the situation—and this one was pretty grim—they would get through it together.

Susan was able, amid her own shock and concern, to keep the perspective that this was a temporary situation that would be forgotten in time. She had to act out of faith that this situation would resolve itself and she would make the best decisions she could. She encouraged Shelly to continue to attend school, walk proud, and confront her ex. By supporting her daughter rather than just punishing her, Susan taught Shelly that it takes courage to stand strong, but it is the best option we have. Susan shared with her daughter that true friends will stick by you when gossip or scandal run amok, while fake friends will fall by the wayside, which can also be difficult. The confidence Susan displayed (faked, in many ways) helped both of them cross the initial bridges. Then she could lean back a little and help Shelly own up to her part in this mistake and learn from her actions.

THE IMPORTANCE OF TAKING RISKS

Part of an adolescent's job is taking risks, learning boundaries, forming opinions, and developing perspective based on the experience of taking the risk. It can be nerve-racking to support your child in taking risks, so if you can't wrap your head around encouraging it, just know it's what she should do and try not to get in her way. This exploration of the world will help to define who she is and what drives her.

Taking risks can look different at different ages and in different situations. To one teen, posting a political meme might feel like stepping out on a ledge, while to another, speaking up in class might be a huge hurdle. Your child will have many small and large opportunities to take risks, and you should help her weigh when she should move ahead and when she should shy away. Talk to your child about her experiences, her decisions, and the outcomes. What has she learned? She will rely on her experiences and the conversations with you when she is faced with the bigger risks of whether or not to drink or how much to drink, whether or not to get in the car with a friend who is high, whether or not to cheat, and so on. And the deeper your conversations go, the more options your child will see, understanding that there is not necessarily one right and wrong decision for every situation. And what seems like the right decision may, in retrospect, have been wrong. Kids have to be able to make the best possible decision in the moment, and they need to reflect on all kinds of past decisions to help them with future decisions.

DEVELOPING VULNERABILITY

Kids don't know everything about their parents, and that's normal. That said, it's helpful for our kids to know more about us than we may show them. Our children often have a two-dimensional image of us, in part because we only share select pieces of ourselves and our past. I was once admonishing my kids for arguing, and I said something about how my sisters included me and made me feel welcome even though I was the younger one. My son responded with, "Well, that's because you had the perfect fairy-tale childhood."

I was taken aback and laughed. I certainly didn't. I had a good childhood, but I'd never considered it perfect. It's important for our kids to see our imperfections—to know we have insecurities, concerns, sadness, frustration. We don't want to harp on our troubles because we don't want adult problems to weigh on them, but it's good for our kids to see us in our own struggles every now and then.

To be vulnerable is to open yourself up, knowing there is a possibility of being hurt. Author and researcher Brené Brown points out that we often feel that the way we do something or view a matter is the way it "should" be done or viewed. And anything contrary to our perspective may feel like an attack or judgment on our own choices. Addressing self-doubt allows us to embrace vulnerability and work toward what we hope for our kids, and to remove ourselves from the notion that there is only one way, or a right way. When we love ourselves for who we are, we teach our children to do the same.

Think about the experiences that have defined you, made you more resilient, and developed strength in you—then share them with your children. Those experiences are not the fairy tale times when things turned out perfectly—they are the gritty, stuck-in-the-mud-and-I-might-give-up experiences. They are the "edge experiences," where you were in a difficult spot but mustered the guts to bear through it till the end, coming out on the other side feeling beat up but stronger.

Avoid using shame or shaming your child directly. Shame doesn't have a place in discipline or learning, as it conveys a sense of disappointment in the person rather than the act. This contributes to lower self-confidence and self-esteem. Raise your child to aim for self-fulfillment and satisfaction rather than to strive for perfection. Teach that falling short of expectations, though it sometimes incurs consequences, is a part of learning and growing.

ADVOCACY AND STANDING UP

While we'd like to think our child would always advocate for another child being targeted, it's much easier to be a bystander, and it's much more in a teen's nature than taking a stand. Don't expect your child to always make a strong decision in the face of adversity. Model advocacy in front of your child and

Remember that your child's behavior is most likely normal. He may be trying on some new hats and testing boundaries. Avoid labeling him a bully or a victim, as that can carry a stigma that will last longer than the events.

If you're concerned that your child may be the target of bullying, look for some of the typical signs:

Is he more moody, withdrawn, sad, anxious, or irritable?

Does he seem to be checking his social media accounts more often than before?

Is he clearing his history on his devices?

Has his self-esteem taken a hit?

Do you notice any issues with substance abuse?

Have his eating or sleeping habits changed?

Is he nervous to go to school or an activity?

Is he asking to change his schedule?

Has he been losing many items?

Does he appear to have an increased number of injuries?

Have his friendships changed drastically?

If you're concerned your child may be expressing bullying behavior, look for some of the typical signs:

Does he seem overly aggressive to peers or adults?

Is he acting defiant?

Has he received many discipline referrals from school?

Does he appear to have trouble with anger management?

Does he get frustrated easily?

Does he lack empathy for others?

Does he boast often?

Does he struggle with criticism?

Does he require a lot of attention?

Does he easily resort to name-calling?

Does he play the blame game rather than accept responsibility?

Is he overly competitive?

Is he himself being bullied?

identify injustices when you see them, both locally and in the media. Help your child practice advocacy that is not directly related to him (like joining a protest for a national movement) to help take the stigma out of being strong and proud in front his friends. With enough conversation and support, your child will learn to stand tall, no matter the situation. When injustices hit closer to home—like when he sees another kid being targeted in the hallway at school—he'll be better prepared to act in accordance with his beliefs.

Help your child build assertive behavior that will lead to brave actions. Assertiveness can sometimes be equated with nastiness or bossiness. Even some adults refrain from being assertive in the hope of appearing polite or avoiding confrontation. Teach your child the power of assertiveness, and show her how to assert herself when it's easy and, eventually, when it's hard. Role-play with your child so she feels armed with the right words. Practice using sound reasoning with small topics, so she is sure of her own convictions before entering a tricky situation. Encourage good physical posture, which can support confidence.

Your child will most likely experience both sides of bullying in her lifetime—as you likely have, as well. The question becomes how we react to the situation. Conversations about advocacy can also help the child who feels targeted. It's important to help your child understand that she has power in either situation, and can rise above, no matter the choices she has made along the way. The best defense against bullying is inner confidence, and you can help to support that by providing a strong foundation at home.

Most instances of bullying can be resolved by the kids. Be aware of red flags, however, and deal with the situation head on. Don't be afraid of labels or that your child will be scarred for life. If you teach your child to stand up and advocate for herself, she will learn how to deal with future situations. That doesn't mean you should sit idly by—offer to help and see what your child needs or wants. Role-play with her if she wants to confront the person or talk with a counselor at school. If you're dealing with a more serious situation, seek assistance through the school and/or get a referral for a counselor or therapist from your pediatrician.

Bias, discrimination, and judgment are natural human reactions distilled from our beliefs, world experience, and early history. Our biases originate in the stories we learn of our own family, religion, and history, and from our own experience. This does not mean that these thoughts or opinions cannot change or that we have to act according to them. We can always recognize our judgments, question them, and then replace those ideas with new ones. The first step is building awareness, the second step is questioning, and the third is rebuilding our judgments. The conversation starters and prompts in this chapter will walk through these steps, offering specific ways to address them with your child.

Joining together to model and promote advocacy is the best way to teach it. It's best if actions for advocacy are your child's idea, but these may not come up naturally. If that's the case, have a conversation with your child about what he wants to support. The cause could be political or social, or just something fun. Does your kid love dogs? Then volunteer for a local rescue agency and learn about what you can do at a bigger level as you get more involved.

While writing this book, there was yet another tragic school shooting. This one was different, in that kids from the school began to speak out and protest, making a case for stronger gun control. It was incredible to see how quickly and effectively this group was able to connect with other youth and organizations across the country, and even the world, to band together in support of a common concern. Whatever your beliefs on this specific issue, moments like these point to ways each person can make a difference—and you can use examples from history, as well as current events, to show your child the power that advocacy can have in changing the world.

GROWTH MINDSET

As we discussed in Chapter 1, we can help kids develop their abilities by encouraging a growth mindset, a belief that talents can be developed through hard work. If a child believes his abilities are limited, he has a fixed mindset and is less likely to work to develop his abilities and potential. As parents, we can support a growth mindset in our kids and encourage them to develop their abilities. How your child sees himself can affect the way he acts. Experiencing failure can help to promote a growth mindset—a single failure is an opportunity to show your child that his abilities are not static and that, while he may face a challenge, he can overcome it. Adopting a growth mindset will help your child persist in the face of challenges or failures and understand more deeply the importance of process.

Kids, from birth, are driven and persistent. For no preset reward, they learn to walk, talk, and manipulate things with their hands. They want to communicate

DEVELOPING A GROWTH MINDSET

If your child demonstrates a fixed mindset, you can help to change her thinking and support growth in her abilities. Here are a few ways to support the development of a growth mindset:

Model it!

Teach your child about brain development and how it works.

Praise effort and not just achievement.

Use mistakes as teachable moments.

Face fears and don't run away from challenges.

See the value in challenges.

and be a part of the world. When they perceive challenges and obstacles as negative, they begin to doubt themselves and set their own internal limits.

There are specific ways you can encourage growth mindset in your child, and one of the key ways is through modeling it yourself. Embrace challenges, talk about your own frustrations and persistence, and encourage determination in your children. Try to use active and reassuring language:

"That sounds hard. What can I do to support you as you try?"

Encourage your kids to face a challenge. "Tough break" or "Some people just aren't good at _____" are comments that set low expectations and support a fixed mindset.

A HEALTHY SENSE OF COMPETITION

Competition is natural, and a healthy competitive sense and practice should be widely encouraged. Competition can get a bad rap for causing unsportsmanlike behavior and for pitting people against one another. Some parents worry that encouraging competition pushes their kids too hard or sets a bad example by putting winning above all else. With a healthy and realistic approach, competition creates a sense of drive and helps kids develop persistence and resilience. Competition can help kids learn the art of winning and losing graciously. Your child won't always win in life—in a lifetime, we all experience losing in small and big ways. Your child may not ace every test, may get cut from the school play, or may be rejected from a college. And as kids get older, they confront bigger losses with bigger consequences. Allowing them to face competition at a young age helps them learn how to rise above challenges.

Don't think of encouraging competition as throwing your kid to the wolves, but as offering her opportunities to compare herself to others with a goal of improving her own performance. As when you encourage a growth mindset, praise your child for effort and practice, and support her personal growth along the journey. Competitions can be light and fun—a game of Monopoly with the family, while low-stakes in the "real world," can offer lots of chances for boasting and trash talk, setting up a chance to talk about what is and is not appropriate.

Above all, when it comes to competition, help your child to see that rising to the challenge is better than running away. As we strive to parent with hope rather than fear, we should encourage our kids to live in the same way. This doesn't mean we don't feel the fear, but that we acknowledge it and face it.

RAISING CONTRIBUTING MEMBERS OF SOCIETY

After talking with thousands of parents, I have found that the overwhelming majority want their children to be happy as adults—and that, in their minds, means independence and the ability to sustain meaningful relationships. In order to achieve this, we need to allow opportunities for kids to experience independence in bite-size pieces as they grow. Think of the parenting long game as raising a contributing member of society. But we need to balance that with the here and now; while future considerations are important, we must also recognize that kids are not fully developed, and we need to ensure their safety and well-being. Look at opportunities for independence as a set of graduating steps, which offer teachable moments all along the way.

Just as you encouraged your toddler to dress herself, make her bed, or pour her own milk, let your adolescent start to do things on her own, such as plan her schedule, keep track of her grades, or find a job. Look for opportunities big and small. Ask your child's opinion and respect her choices. If your son wants to go to a party and you don't know the parents, talk to him about your concerns and together come up with a game plan so he can do what he feels ready for. If your daughter is struggling in school, ask her what she thinks she needs rather than simply signing her up for a tutor. Giving your child choice and independence helps to build the trust between you.

Sometimes your first reaction may be to step in and make a decision or nix a request. If you can, resist that urge. If you find yourself making snap judgments, use some reflective practice to identify those tendencies and try to change the behavior moving forward. Make a concerted effort before saying no to at least ask your child why he is making the request—why is it important to him? This minor shift in your behavior opens up a world of possibilities to your adolescent and allows him a voice and ownership of his decisions.

Inspiration

During brave conversations:

Show and acknowledge vulnerability.

Stand up for your child by standing by him as he stands.

Support and model a growth mindset.

Look for opportunities to foster courage.

Make your home a safe and comfortable place to talk.

Let your child know she can go to you no matter what—all subjects are okay.

We live in an ever-busy world where we and our children are overcommitted and are expected to multitask throughout our days. But multitasking is not fully efficient, because with every bit of attention we give one task, we take attention away from another. Our children see this juggling act and experience it themselves. Help them to focus on one task at a time and consider outside distractions. Teach them to make choices that may be unpopular or might delay gratification. For a teen, something as simple as not checking his phone constantly can feel like an act of courage because it's not the way other kids behave.

Courage takes strength, and it can come to us through small decisions, like sitting with someone new in the school cafeteria, and build into bigger decisions, like writing a letter to congress. In the beginning of this chapter we noted that we can't expect our kids to always make the right decisions, but we can hold them responsible for their actions. By doing this, and by talking through their decisions with them, we can help them to find their own way to courage.

The Brave Project

ACTIVITY 1: EXPLORE COLLEGE

Often, the college conversation starts when kids are young, and as more and more people ask your child about his plans he will feel more pressure. There is a lot to be done to prepare for college, but your child should try to enjoy the application process—college should be a fun next step.

Let your child lead the process as much as possible—this will result in a better fit in the end. If your child is planning to go to college, start exploring the choices and thinking about the process before he must begin to narrow his search (which usually starts around the junior year of high school).

First, talk with your child about the kinds of colleges he is interested in (big or small, urban or rural, Division 1 or Division 3, etc.). Consider your funding options and any financial help you might need to apply for. Compose a list of questions and make an appointment with the college counselor at your child's school to get an idea of the colleges that might fit these parameters, as well as what you and your child need to do to officially begin the process. Be open-minded and don't invest too much talk in one college at the outset. If you can, set up some tours at different types of colleges and note what your child is drawn to. Now that you've explored, you should be able to narrow your list to the types of schools and settings he is interested in, but continue to keep the selection broad until the semester before your child is ready to apply.

ACTIVITY 2: LABEL-MAKING

Often, children hear kids and adults around them make strong conclusions about themselves such as, "I am smart, dumb, average, pretty, athletic, clumsy, dopey, funny." You might make a wrong turn in the car and, in front of your child, exclaim, "Argh, I'm so stupid!" when in reality you just made a wrong turn and that mistake doesn't reflect your general knowledge or skill.

While we cannot fully avoid labels, teach your child to define herself in a variety of ways and help her understand that she will continue to grow and develop into the person she will be. Ask your child what labels she would use to define herself. Then offer some labels you would apply to yourself. Don't be afraid to use some negative ones if they come up—even Mary Poppins is just "practically" perfect. Now ask your child which labels she's proud of and which she's not so proud of. Share your thoughts on your labels, too.

ACTIVITY 3: TELL A STORY—WHEN WERE YOU AFRAID?

Share a memory of a time you were truly afraid, offering details such as how you felt, what you were wearing, and so on. Dig deep into the emotion of the memory and share honestly what made you afraid. Ask your child to share a moment he was truly afraid, then talk about what you or your child could have done differently in those circumstances. Show your child that there are alternative decisions and paths we can take.

CONVERSATION STARTERS AND PROMPTS

Here are some prompts and talking points for starting a brave conversation with your child:

ADVOCACY AND EMPOWERMENT

Talk about interests and identify areas where you can make a difference—through volunteering for an organization close to your heart, for example, or perhaps by becoming politically active. It's not always easy, but if you and your child feel passionate about an issue, then go out there and support the effort.

"What organizations are you interested in?"

"I'd like us to start volunteering together—can you think of anything you'd like to do? Here are some ideas I came up with...."

"I noticed you're talking a lot about [insert topic] and I wondered if there was something we could do to learn more."

When talking about awareness of biases, consider your own beliefs and how they affect your decisions. Start by acknowledging that we all carry our own biases, so having a bias is natural and doesn't make you a bad person. However, make it clear that it does impact how you act and who you interact with. And, in fact, some people may harass or discriminate against others, acting on their own biases.

"Sometimes, people think they are better than other people because of their race, ethnicity, sex, sexual orientation, or religion. Is that something you've noticed? When?"

"What are some of the beliefs you have about people who are different from yourself?"

"Where do you think you got some of these ideas? Were there stories that you heard? Things that you saw or experienced?"

"Are you scared or nervous around certain types of people?"

"Do you feel like you can only be friends with certain types of people?"

Questioning your belief system is the second step in understanding your own biases. These are questions that you and your child can answer together.

"Are you curious about people who are different from you? What do you want to know about them?"

"Are differences between people a positive or a negative thing? In what way? Please give some examples of both."

"Have you judged someone too quickly and found out that you were wrong in your judgment? What did you learn from this experience?"

Rebuilding our judgments and dismantling our biases is the third step in the process. Understanding where we have been and where we want to go is a lifelong goal. Allowing ourselves to take a hard look at how we view and treat other people can be a difficult step in becoming more compassionate and developing deeper connections with others.

"How can we neutralize bias and judgment of others?"

"What would the benefit of this action be?"

"How can you develop more compassion and empathy for others?"

BULLYING AND BEING BULLIED

Be honest and open with your child about bullying. Remember, much of what kids do is normal, so don't panic. But also be clear about your hopes and what your kid can do if she finds herself on either side of bullying.

"I got a call from school today—do you have sense of what it was about?"

"It seems like you and ____ aren't friendly anymore. Is that true?"

"Are there times you don't feel safe?"

"I read about a case of bullying today and want to share it with you."

EMOTIONAL HEALTH AND ANXIETY

Check in and take your child's emotional temperature regularly. Have him express his emotions in words. Regularly checking in with your child will give you a baseline of how he is doing and will help you determine if he is out of his "normal" range and needs more attention or assistance.

"Emotions are like colors of the rainbow. Maybe red is anger, blue is sadness, pink is joy, and purple is anxiety. You also may feel more than one emotion at a time. What are you feeling right now?"

"What does that feeling make you want to do?"

"Think about how our behavior feeds into our feelings. For example, if we are sad, we may feel like sleeping all day, but we need to think about whether that behavior (sleeping) feeds the feeling we don't want. What behavior would feed a feeling of happiness?"

"Strong emotions can be scary sometimes, and certain feelings like deep sadness or anxiety should be shared with an adult. Have you ever felt that way? Have you known another person who felt that way?"

"You seem different from your usual self. Do you sense yourself changing? How?"

"Do you ever feel like talking to anyone else? What makes you feel more comfortable about sharing your feelings? How can I help?"

"When you get stressed, what does it look like? How do you know you are stressed? How do you handle it? What are some healthy ways to cope with stress?"

Stress can often be handled by talking and expressing yourself. If you feel your child is struggling with stress or anxiety or another mental health issue, ask your pediatrician for some support and a possible referral to a mental health professional. While you don't want to panic, you do want to address concerns as quickly as you can.

INDEPENDENCE AND TRANSITIONS

Your child should know that part of your job is to help her grow up into a self-sufficient person. And hopefully you've been giving her opportunities to demonstrate responsibility. Continue to support her independence by talking about her hopes and dreams.

"What do you want to be when you grow up?"

"What do you think you'll do when you grow up?"

HELPING YOUR ANXIOUS CHILD

These three easy techniques can help a child (or an adult!) emotionally "unhook"—let go of anxious states:

1. **Breathing.** Breathe in and think a positive thought in the moment: "Hello, I am feeling okay. I can do this." Breathe out and think of anything you want to let go of: "Goodbye, worries about my performance."

2. **Worry stones, fidget toys, glass stones.** Kids who worry really like to have something physical with them to rub or touch when they feel anxiety-provoking thoughts spinning or returning. One patient I worked with loved the sheepskin rugs in my office, so we cut a piece from the rug for him to carry in his pocket as a "security blanket." This piece of fabric created a great sense of security for him, and he was excited that he could take it with him everywhere. This action of tuning in to something physical is grounding. It helps bring us back to the present focus, which increases our locus of control—the feeling that we can influence the outcome of events.

3. **Deep hugs, compression.** This is another grounding technique. When people worry, they tend to talk about feeling fragmented and coming "undone." A deep hug or gentle presses on the shoulders helps the body to literally feel more grounded to the earth. This physical sensation can stimulate the parasympathetic nervous system, which induces calm within the body.

"What kind of job or role would best reflect who you are?"

If college is an assumed plan, talk about it early and often and note any concerns or limitations. If your child doesn't want to go or doesn't want to go right away, help map out alternative plans. Consider talking with the counselor at your school for some added support.

"Have you met with your counselor about how to start looking at colleges? What did she have to say?"

"Want to take a day trip and look at some schools?"

"What does your ideal college look like? Why?"

"What's important to you to have at college (sports, liberal arts, a specific department, club teams, an urban feel...)?"

MENTAL HEALTH

Mental health is one of the most difficult subjects for parents to bring up with their children. Asking your child to describe mental hurdles, hardships, and emotions can bring up your own insecurities and feelings of helplessness. We never want to think our kids are in pain, but it happens and there is always a way out of it. We need to help our kids understand that we are here to help with whatever comes their way.

"You seem anxious. Can you describe the feeling?"

"Everyone feels out of control sometimes. When do you feel like that? Does the feeling come on quickly?"

"Have you ever felt like you have an inside pain that will never go away?"

"Where do you envision yourself in a year? What about in five years?"

"What kind of support do you feel you have? Who could you go to for more? What kind of support do you need?"

Encourage competition and celebrate the wins, but always be mindful of the reason for competition. Focus on learning from losses and frustrations.

"Tell me more about why you think it went that way."

Respond with metaphors to help your child interpret an experience. Or use a story from your past.

"What was the experience like for you?"

"I'm glad you tried that. How did trying that feel?"

DEALING WITH DEPRESSION

Sometimes, when people have depression, they don't see that every situation is temporary, that the pain is temporary. When I work with people who are in emotional pain, I tell them that the "inside" or emotional injury is like a broken bone. This is a very useful metaphor for emotional, psychological injury. When you break your leg, you have to go the hospital, get a cast, learn to hobble around with a crutch, and then you can go home. But eventually, you will learn to walk again with lots of help and support. "Inside" or emotional hurts are very similar. When you feel deeply sad, you need to seek a doctor's help, you need lots of support initially, you may need medication, and you need time to heal your hurt. It is very important, when you feel emotional hurt, that you seek help and talk about how you feel because, unlike a broken bone, parents and others can't tell how you feel by looking at your body.

"Is there anything you would do differently?"

"What did you learn from the experience?"

VULNERABILITY

Share with your child a time when you have felt compromised professionally or personally. Show her that this doesn't make you weak, but is part of who you have become as a result of the experience.

> "Have you ever felt compromised like that? What did you do? Would you have done anything differently?"

Share a time when you were brave.

> "What does it mean to you to be brave? Have you ever had to be brave? Can you tell me more about it?"

CONVERSATION IN ACTION

Your seventeen-year-old son nervously approaches you and confides that he is not interested in attending college. College has been the plan—or so you thought—and you are taken off guard. He's taken the SAT, sat through the counseling sessions at school, and even gone on a few college tours without ever hinting that this might not be his next step. Now that you think of it, he has shown some doubt that he'll get into a few schools you've mentioned, but you cannot recall any time he said he wasn't going to college.

First, take a deep breath—remember that no decision is final. On top of that, a decision has not been made. Most importantly, your son needs to develop on his own, and if he's not ready or interested in college, forcing him to go could backfire. See his reluctance as an opportunity for a deeper discussion.

Start with a debrief. Acknowledge what he's said and validate his opinion and concerns. Feel free to share your shock.

"This is new information to me. You've taken me off guard. I might need some time to process this. I'm really glad you are sharing this with me now. Have you been thinking about this for a while?"

If you need some time, take it. When you're ready to come back to the conversation, talk about where the decision is coming from:

"You seem confident in your decision. Are you?"

"This feels like a shift in direction. Did something inspire this shift or did I miss some signals along the way?"

"Do you have fears about the application process or leaving home?"

"Is attending a college close to home or taking a few courses at a local community college an option you'd consider?"

"Have you talked with your counselor at all? What is his opinion?"

If your son feels firm in his decision, rather than trying to change his opinion, try to get him to think about his own decision-making process. Is there anything else to consider? Talk about what his next steps could look like.

"What are your short-term and long-term goals?"

"What options do you have if you don't go to college?"

"Would college be an option for the long-term, in your opinion?"

Your son is growing up and can, in fact, legally make his own decisions starting at age eighteen. Ideally, you will maintain a strong relationship with him through adulthood, and if that is the goal, then taking a strong stand on college and coercing him to attend by dangling financial (or other) incentives is not the most productive option. It might lead to a college degree, but it won't lead to his ultimate independence and might cause an irreparable rift between you.

"TO LISTEN IS TO LEAN IN SOFTLY WITH A WILLINGNESS TO BE CHANGED BY WHAT WE HEAR."

MARK NEPO

CONCLUSION

I mentioned to a friend of mine that I was finishing the editing process of this book, and she asked me about it, noting that she was desperate to connect with her teen daughter. She had many great things to say about her daughter—as a junior in high school, her daughter was already captain of the soccer team and the lacrosse team, president of the student body, a straight-A student taking four advanced placement classes, and looking at a list of elite colleges hoping to recruit her. But, the mother confided in a guarded voice, "...she isn't very nice. Everyone thinks she's so great, and she is, but she's mean. She doesn't think she needs to be parented, that she's got it all figured out already."

This mother felt she had spent the last seventeen years raising an ungrateful child, and she and her husband were at their wits' end. After she'd vented, it was time to inquire a bit. How long had she felt this way? Was this a new issue or something that had been building? I learned that mother and daughter had actually been quite close, and it was fairly clear to me, as an outsider, that the teen's behavior was a natural part of growing up. She was becoming more independent and flexing her wings a bit. It was time to celebrate all the young woman had achieved, but also, more importantly, who she is. It was also time to remind her of some of the expectations her mother had and to reestablish those. This teen had her own pressures—high achievers can feel that they have an impossible task being as good as everyone expects them to be. What both mother and daughter really needed was to reconnect.

Writing this book has been our own adventure, as we learned more about the intersection between the science of psychology and education and the art of parenting. While working on the book, we've leaned on both our professional wisdom and our personal experience to fill the pages with ideas and activities to help you navigate this very intersection.

During the planning and writing of *The Parenting Project,* we spent a lot of time thinking about our own conversations with our kids—analyzing how often we started our talks, how many started without prompting, and how we've had to shift the tone or stop and start again when things go amiss. We've shared the content with our children and invited their input. We are grateful for their contributions, but even more for their participation because it is the act of conversation that inspired this book and helped to establish a bond with our children. Conversation starts as a way to relate, but then lays a foundation of topics, interests, opinions, and stories that bind us moving forward.

There is no one way to talk with your child, and as you develop your conversation style you will learn what works best. Nourish the conversations you have with patience and perseverance. Remember, each child is different and relationships are different, so what works with one of your children may not work with another. And when things slow, turn to this book as a companion and get the conversation rolling again.

The conversations you have with your kids will strengthen your relationship but will also help them learn more about you and about themselves. Your children will be stronger as a result, better able to build relationships of all kinds because of the time you take to talk with them.

"CONVERSATION STARTS AS A WAY TO RELATE, BUT THEN LAYS A FOUNDATION OF TOPICS, INTERESTS, OPINIONS, AND STORIES THAT BIND US MOVING FORWARD."

SUGGESTED RESOURCES

ORGANIZATIONS

American Academy of Pediatrics
www.aap.org

American Foundation for Suicide Prevention
www.afsp.org

American Psychological Association
www.apa.org

Center for Parent and Teen Communication
http://parentandteen.com

Challenge Success
www.challengesuccess.org

Common Sense Media
www.commonsensemedia.org

National Alliance on Mental Illness
www.nami.org

National Suicide Prevention Lifeline
www.suicidepreventionlifeline.org

Natural High
www.naturalhigh.org

PBS Parents
www.pbs.org/parents/education/going-to-school/social/

True Colors: Sexual Minority Youth and Family Services
www.ourtruecolors.org

BOOKS

Alone Together: Why We Expect More from Technology and Less from Each Other, by Sherry Turkle

The Blessing of a B Minus: Using Jewish Teachings to Raise Resilient Teenagers, by Wendy Mogel, Ph.D.

Bully Nation: Why America's Approach to Childhood Aggression is Bad for Everyone, by Susan Eva Porter, Ph.D.

Daring Greatly: How the Courage to Be Vulnerable Transforms the Way We Live, Love, Parent, and Lead, by Brené Brown, Ph.D., L.M.S.W.

How to Talk to Your Kids about Your Divorce: Healthy, Effective Communication Techniques for Your Changing Family, by Dr. Samantha Rodman

How to Talk So Teens Will Listen and Listen So Teens Will Talk, by Adele Faber and Elaine Mazlish

Mindset: The New Psychology of Success, by Carol S. Dweck, Ph.D.

Not So Fast: Parenting Your Teen Through the Dangers of Driving, by Tim Hollister and Pam Shadel Fischer

A Parent's Guide to Building Resilience in Children and Teens: Giving Your Child Roots and Wings, by Kenneth R. Ginsburg, M.D., M.S. Ed.

Raising Kids to Thrive: Balancing Love with Expectations and Protection with Trust, by Kenneth R. Ginsburg, M.D., M.S. Ed.

Screen-Smart Parenting: How to Find Balance and Benefit in Your Child's Use of Social Media, Apps, and Digital Devices, by Jodi Gold, M.D.

A Secure Base: Parent-Child Attachment and Healthy Human Development, by John Bowlby

A Survival Guide to Parenting Teens: Talking to Your Kids About Sexting, Drinking, Drugs, and Other Things That Freak You Out, by Joani Geltman, M.S.W.

Talking to Your Kids About Sex: Turning "the Talk" into a Conversation for Life, by Dr. Laura Berman

Teach Your Children Well: Parenting for Authentic Success, by Madeline Levine, Ph.D.

Uncommon Sense for Parents with Teenagers, by Mike Riera, Ph.D.

Verbal First Aid: Help Your Kids Heal from Fear and Pain—and Come Out Strong, by Judith Simon Prager, Ph.D., and Judith Acosta, L.C.S.W., C.H.T.

ABOUT THE AUTHORS

Dr. Amy Alamar has worked in the field of education as a classroom teacher, professor, parent educator, and education reformer for more than fifteen years. She has conducted significant research in the areas of student stress, parent involvement, learning and instruction, curriculum design and implementation, and using education research to support engagement and communication.

In late 2014, Dr. Alamar published her first book, *Parenting for the Genius: Developing Confidence in Your Parenting through Reflective Practice* (For the Genius Press). A comprehensive guide to becoming the most thoughtful and confident parent possible, the book includes anecdotes and details relating to the guidance and support of children throughout their formative years. Dr. Alamar hosted *Parenting from the Trenches* on Yellowbrick.me, is a contributing author to the Disney parenting website *Babble* and the psychology blog *Hey Sigmund,* and co-hosts the podcast *Parenting Beyond the Headlines.*

Dr. Alamar worked as the director of learning and instruction at Gooru, designing and implementing digital curriculum for K-12 schools. Before that, she served as the schools program director for Challenge Success at Stanford University, where she oversaw programming for member schools and conducted professional development for middle and high school faculty and parent education presentations.

As a frequent speaker to parent groups, Dr. Alamar focuses on a wide range of topics, including student stress and well-being, raising digital natives in the information age, and parenting kids with character. She also conducts faculty development workshops that focus on engagement with learning, professional communication, and curriculum design. In 2016, she was an invited guest of Michelle Obama at the White House for a conversation about kids' health.

Dr. Alamar is married and the mother of three children, who she learns from and enjoys each and every day. She is a resident of Avon, Connecticut, where she serves on the board of the Watkinson School and the Avon Education Foundation, dedicated to promoting and enhancing excellence in education. You can learn more about her www.amyalamar.com.

Dr. Kristine Schlichting, Ph.D., aka Dr. K, is an innovator, entrepreneur, expert problem solver, and change agent fusing together the principles of psychology, organizational behavior, coaching, and wellness. She is a licensed psychologist in the state of Connecticut and earned her doctorate in psychology from the University of Connecticut. She also received specialized training in both cognitive-behavioral and solution-focused therapy during her masters degree training at the University of Wisconsin-Madison. She is CEO of Hopewell Health Solutions (HHS), a multi-disciplinary psychology group practice in Glastonbury, Connecticut.

Over the past ten years, Dr. Schlichting has "broken the box" of traditional talk therapy to develop a new model (i-therapy) for change which is based on recent developments in neuroscience. Guiding her staff in this treatment ensures that every HHS therapist's work is rooted in this practice. In addition, Dr. Schlichting provides individual, group, and family therapy for children, adolescents, and adults.

Dr. Schlichting has conducted research in the areas of anxiety, group dynamics, and video self-modeling. Her innovative research has been published in various articles and books. She travels throughout New England providing consultation, seminars, and trainings for conferences, medical offices, schools, and corporations. Her trainings are multimedia, interactive, and goal-focused, and all content is directed toward efficient and relevant implementation. Through her concierge clinical work with executives throughout the country, Dr. Schlichting has been named as a top provider by the Health Network Foundation, a private organization aimed at connecting CEOs and business leaders with exceptional medical providers.

Dr. Schlichting is a fierce advocate committed to helping all children and adults reach their full potential. She also is a mother to a child with dyslexia, dysgraphia, ADHD, and learning disabilities, so she understands firsthand the struggle many parents face. In her free time, she enjoys adrenaline-filled adventures with her family.

INDEX

A

Advocacy and empowerment
conversation starters and
prompts, 181–183
developing, 171, 173–175
Ainsworth, Mary, 88
Anxiety
conversation starters and
prompts, 183–184
tips for reducing, 185
Assault conversation starters and
prompts, 138
Assertiveness building, 173–175
Assumptions, danger of making,
38
Attachment theory, 88

B

Blink (Gladwell), 74
Body image conversation,
157–158
Body language. See Nonverbal
language
Boundaries, pushing, 20, 170
Bowlby, John, 88
Brave conversations
about, 48–49
in action, 188–189
developing vulnerability and,
170–171
explore college activity, 180
label-making activity, 180–181
starters and prompts, 181–184,
186–188
story about being afraid
activity, 181
tips for, 179
Brown, Brené, 92, 171
Bullying
conversations about, 174, 183
signs of, 172–173

C

Character building, 154–155
Character conversations
about, 47–48
in action, 165–167
body image talk activity,
157–158
giving examples, 148–149

practicing mindfulness activity,
156–157
share a lesson activity, 156
sharing morals and values,
149–150
social media and, 151
starters, 159–163, 165
tips for, 156
Competition, developing healthy
sense of, 177–178
Control issue, mitigating, 41
Conversation Checklist, 68–69
Conversations
Child's, with professionals or
other adults, 62, 63,
76
Child's refusal to participate,
60, 61
confrontational, 62–63
cues for, 53
exchange nature of, 39
finding right environment for,
26, 28
as foundation of relationships,
51
as habit, 21, 51–54
as key to interdependence,
9–10
as process, 31, 78–79
prompts for, 80–81
restarting, 56
urgent, 61, 62
using to clarify perspectives,
38–39
See also specific conversations
Crisis, kids in, red flags for, 126,
128–129
Cutting behaviors, conversation
starters and prompts, 139

D

Dangerous conversations
about, 44–47
in action, 142–145
being nonjudgmental, 131
finding child's natural high
activity, 136
open-ended questions, 132
red flags, 126, 128–129
risk taking and emotional type
activity, 132–136

scary news activity, 136
starters and prompts, 136–142
substance abuse, 137
tips for, 131
Daring Greatly (Brown), 92
Dating, 90–91
Decision-making
conversation starters, 159
development of ability, 40,
150
as process, 126–127, 129–130
risk-taking conversation
starters and prompts,
187
taking responsibility for
actions and, 147–149
talking about risk-taking, 170
teaching, 178
understanding consequences,
150
Depression, dealing with,
187–188
Digital communications, 91–92,
151
Diversity, conversation starters
and prompts, 117–118
Divorce/separation conversations
in action, 120–123
starters and prompts, 118
Driving, conversation starters and
prompts, 139–140
Dweck, Carol, 30–31

E

Education and life skills,
conversation starters,
160–161
Emotional health and anxiety,
conversation starters and
prompts, 183–184
Emotions
acknowledging and validating
child's, 20, 38, 76
brain and, 73
child's emotional type, 94–96,
132–136
considering own, 77–78
conversation starters and
prompts, 99
displaying, in safe
environments, 37

expressing, 41
grief, 87, 102
importance of, 84
internalizing child's negative, 38–39
naming, 78, 86, 97
shutting down and, 56
signs of onset of moods, 37–38
Empathy, expressing, 41–42
Environment
checking for comfort, 68, 69
displaying emotions in safe, 37
finding right, 26, 28
possible comfortable, 70–72
urgent conversations and, 70
Expectations
letting go of, 77
making clear, 45
modeling, 58
setting high, 47

F
Family, conversation starters and prompts, 99–100
Family mottos, using, 33
Family time, dinner as, 53
Fear, conversation starters and prompts, 119
Feelings. *See* Emotions
Fixed mindset, 30
Flexibility
conversation outcomes and, 66
taking lead from child, 54–55
in thinking, 43
Flow, going with, 55
Fluidity, 55
Friendships
conversation in action, 103–105
conversation starters and prompts, 100
importance of, 88–89

G
Gender and gender identity, conversation starters and prompts, 119
Gladwell, Malcom, 74
Gratitude, practicing, 153
Grief, stages of, 87

Grief and loss, conversation starters and prompts, 102
Growth mindset, 30, 31, 176–177

H
Harassment, conversation starters and prompts, 138
Healthy habits, conversation starters, 161
Heart-based conversations
about, 40–42
in action, 103–105
assessing child's emotional type activity, 94–96
checking child's friendships/ romantic involvements activity, 96–97
naming emotions activity, 97
naming feelings, 86
starters and prompts, 99–103
tips for, 93
See also Relationships
Honesty, 111–114
Humility, conversation starters, 162

I
I-therapy, goal of, 14
Identity, conversation starters, 162
Impulse control, learning, 126–127, 129–130
Independence
conversation starters and prompts, 184, 186
desire to shield child and, 65
as goal of parenting, 9
supporting child's, 40
Integrity, conversation starters, 163
Interdependence, 9–10
Intimacy, 89–91, 101

J
Judgmentalness, avoiding, 39, 40, 76, 131

K
Kübler-Ross, Elizabeth, 87

L
Learning styles, understanding own, 29–31

Life experiences, talking about and using lessons from own, 31, 33
Listening
by children, 58
conversation as back-and-forth, 55
mindfully, 77
true, 39

M
Media management, 109–111
Memories, incorporating, 78
Mental health
anxiety, 183–184, 185
conversation starters and prompts, 186
dealing with depression, 187–188
See also Suicide
Metaphors, using, 98–99
Mindfulness, 152–153, 156–157
Minor vices, conversation starters and prompts, 141
Misra, Shalini, 70
Mistakes, as learning opportunities, 58–59, 65, 130–131
Multitasking, 71–72

N
911, when to call, 62
Nonparticipating children
ideas for engaging, 74–75
preparing for, 60
signs of, 61
Nonverbal messaging
checking, 69
confrontational, 72–73
deciphering child's, 41, 74
faking positive, 73
importance of, 74
mirroring, 74
modeling advocacy, 171, 173–175
modeling empathy and coping strategies, 86
modeling expectations, 58
modeling good relationships, 90
modeling values and morals, 149–151

open body posture, 72
    practicing gratitude, 153
    reading child's, 42
    relaxing own, 41

O
Open-ended questions, 77, 132

P
Parent-child Q&A, 22–26
Parents
    examining own hopes, fears,
        concerns, and
        motivations, 21
    personal childhood stories of,
        33–34
    Q&As for interviewing, 22–26
    reactions of, 28–29
Phone, as distraction, 70
Positive, focusing on, 75
Punishments, acknowledgements
    and, 20

R
Relationships
    boundaries and, 92–93, 95
    conversation in action,
        103–105
    deep connections, 92–93
    empathy and, 41
    heart-based conversations
        and, 40–41
    modeling good, 90
    parent-child, sets foundation
        for all other, 88
Risky behaviors, 126
Role-playing
    advocacy conversations, 174,
        175
    as practicing, 77
    uncomfortable conversations,
        44

S
Safe friends, 135
Self-doubt, 171
Self-empathy, demonstrating, 57
Self-image, supporting child's,
    158
Self-love, conversation starters
    and prompts, 102
Setting of conversations.
    See Environment

Sex and sexuality
    age starting having, 115
    conversation environment, 112
    conversation starters and
        prompts, 120
    dating and, 91
    having talk about, 113–116
    intimacy and, 90
    media images of, 110–111
Shutting down, 56
Social media and technology
    conversation in action,
        165–167
    conversation starters, 163
    managing, 151, 164
Spirituality, conversation starters,
    165
Stories, telling, 33–34
Strategies for productive
    conversations, 75–78
Substance abuse
    conversation starters and
        prompts, 128–129, 137
    red flags for, 128–129
Suicide
    conversation in action,
        142–145
    conversation starters and
        prompts, 141–142
    red flags for, 128, 129

T
Tension breakers, yoga, 43
Timing
    checking, 68
    giving child space, 103
    suggestions, 72
Tone of conversation, 68, 69
Tone of voice, 67
Topics
    acknowledging own
        discomfort about, 59
    soliciting, 66–67
    trustworthiness, 27
Transitions. *See* Independence
Trust and trustworthiness
    characteristics of, 27
    conversation starters and
        prompts, 102–103
    intimacy and, 89
    when someone breaks child's,
        32–33

U
Uncomfortable conversations
    about, 42–44
    in action, 120–123
    comfort zone, identifying and
        leaving, 108–109
    having talk about sex activity,
        113–116
    life transitions and, 111
    managing media, 109–111
    movie night activity, 113
    play "I Never" activity, 116–117
    starters and prompts, 117–120
    tips for, 113
Unconditional love, meaning of, 9
Urgent conversations, 70

V
Validation, importance of, 39
Violent threats by child, 127
Vulnerability, developing, 170–171
    conversation starters and
        prompts, 188

X
X-plan, 133

Y
Yoga, 43